INSIDE:

EIGHT VICTIMS:

1. Charles Lafarge
2. The Duchess of Praslin
3. Émile Angelier
4. Séraphine de Pawr
5. Charles Bravo
6. Hippolyte Menaldo
7. Madeleine Grille
8. William Bernays

and the EIGHT ACCUSED:

1. Marie Lafarge
2. The Duke of Praslin
3. Madeleine Smith
4. Edmond de la Pommerais
5. Florence Bravo
6. The Marquis de Nayve
7. Henri Chambige
8. Armand Pelzer

NOTED MURDER MYSTERIES

WALMER BELLES-LETTRES

NOTED MURDER MYSTERIES

by

MARIE BELLOC LOWNDES

ADELAIDE
MICHAEL WALMER
2019

Noted Murder Mysteries first published 1914
under the pseudonym Philip Curtin

This edition published 2019

by

Michael Walmer
9/2 Dahlmyra Avenue
Hamley Bridge
South Australia 5401

ISBN 978-0-6485905-7-6 paperback

"Society is conducted on the assumption
that murder will not be committed."

The Spectator

CONTENTS

INTRODUCTION

THE interest in crime is among the most universal of all interests. It possesses ardent devotees in every class of life, and constitutes the recreation of scholars, statesmen, poets—in fact, of all kinds of people who work with their brains, as well as of many who live by other forms of labour.

But this interest, which is called for convenience an interest in crime, is really an interest only in crimes which are interesting. Great is the number of murders which are committed every year throughout the world, but singularly few of them present features so unusual as to appeal either to the heart or to the intellect. Still fewer crimes have the power of touching both the heart and the intellect, but it is these exceptions of exceptions which are noised abroad all over the world and are studied and re-studied sometimes for generations.

This fascination of crime is acknowledged by numbers of people of all kinds, whom it unites into a sort of freemasonry. They collect books and pamphlets bearing on notable trials, and, unlike most other collectors, they are always ready to share their discoveries with any kindred spirit. There is at least one club with a distinguished membership for what may be called the co-operative study of absorbing cases.

The interest in crime must, indeed, be as old as human nature itself, for that is what it is ultimately based on—the interest of humanity in its own drama. That this interest may transcend that of the greatest works of fiction is periodically demonstrated when some trial seizes the imagination of a whole nation, and the organs of the press vie with one another in publishing every scrap of information even remotely connected with the case. A notable murder trial is in fact a tragedy acted out again before a nation, and the vast audience is keenly alive to every touch of human nature revealed throughout its development.

Even romances which are called immortal are left on the shelf by the children, or at any rate the grandchildren, of those who once delighted in reading them ; but certain historic trials have a longer life. They pass their unsolved riddles on from one generation to another, and such stories of crime will linger in the minds of old people who have forgotten contemporary events which might be thought to have touched them far more nearly.

The student of what may be called, for want
of a better term, "intelligent murder" cannot
but be struck by two facts.

The first is the great part which sex has played
in almost all the famous murder mysteries of the
civilized world. Here there are numerous sub-
divisions. The first and largest is concerned
with every form of illicit love. Again and again
an intelligent, refined, educated woman has
murdered, or attempted to murder, her husband
in order that she might become the legal wife of
her lover—sometimes, be it noted, of her platonic
lover. The intelligent, cultivated, apparently
humane man has again and again murdered, or
tried to murder, his wife because he has fallen
under the domination of another woman. This
is well known, but what is not so generally
realized is the fact that little children are sometimes the innocent cause of such crimes. Often
it has happened that a woman would have gone
away with her lover had she not been unable to
bear the thought of leaving her children, and she
has in consequence been brought to face the
alternative of murdering her husband. The
same thing happens, though much less often,
with a man; even he is sometimes restrained
from leaving his wife by his love for his children,
and is consequently tempted to contemplate her
removal as the easiest solution.

Yet another sub-division is distinguished by jealousy as the paramount motive for murder. Sex jealousy is more common in France than in England, and it inspires the vast majority of French *crimes passionels.*

Next to sex, but certainly a long way after it, comes the influence of money, which is most potent when it is combined with the overmastering motive of sex. By itself, the pecuniary motive, as a rule, produces merely a sordid and generally brutal crime, which presents no feature of interest to the connoisseur.

In the following studies of murder or of attempted murder, I have endeavoured to present in each instance a complete picture, giving due value to its dramatic and romantic elements. It is impossible to do this in a brief space, for it must be remembered that every *cause célèbre* is of enormous length, as anyone who has ever read the transcript of the shorthand notes of such a case can testify.

Severe compression is therefore the first necessity. At the same time, I feel very strongly that the interest of such narratives as these depends primarily on their trustworthiness as presentations of real events in the way in which they actually happened. And so I am particularly anxious to make it clear that the form in

---

which these cases are presented has in no instance been unwarrantably heightened for the sake of effect. Even the titles given to them, which might appear at first sight somewhat fanciful, will be found in each case to be truly descriptive of the essential characteristic. Whatever effect these stories have is derived from their own dramatic qualities. Nothing has been added or invented, and in each case the picture is as accurate as I have known how to make it. The only alteration I have allowed myself is in the names of certain characters who may be still alive, and in these I have employed as the surname some common Christian name other than that of the real person.

Why then, it may be asked, should not the verbatim reports of such trials alone be given? The answer is plain. Full reports are only fitted for, and can only be properly understood by, the specialist. The general reader quickly loses himself in the mass of detail, and is unable without guidance to disentangle what is important.

My function has been twofold. First, to select the essential facts of each case, not from the purely legal point of view, but in their broader aspect as poignant illustrations of human nature. Secondly, what is much more difficult, to present these essential facts in their proper relation to one another. I have ever borne in mind that the absorbing interest of these stories lies in their reality. The actions and the conversations attributed to the characters in each drama are what the people really did and said. The narratives are all directly based on the best sources ; and whenever possible verbatim reports have been used. It should be remembered also that in the French and the Belgian courts " what the soldier said " is not only admitted as evidence but eagerly welcomed.

I have in each case also endeavoured to conceal where my own sympathies lie, preferring to pay the reader the compliment of setting before him all relevant material on either side in order that he may form his own judgment.

With this preface we may now pass on to consider some of the distinguishing features of the cases selected.

The Lafarge case remains the most absorbing and the most baffling of all French murder mysteries, and it is still so regarded by lawyers all over Europe. Two German jurisconsults wrote a long and minutely detailed study of the case, and not very long ago the trial was given out as a thesis to Paris law students. Was Marie Lafarge rightly convicted on the circumstantial evidence, or was she the innocent victim of evidence manufactured to secure her condemnation? Not only France but all Europe took sides on the question, and her trial gave, as we shall see, the first great opportunity of his life to Lachaud, the most famous French advocate of the nineteenth century.

It is a curious and interesting fact that Marie Lafarge was a granddaughter of Philippe Égalité and of Madame de Genlis; she was thus descended in a direct line from Henri Quatre, and through Madame, the mother of the Regent, from Mary Queen of Scots.

The supposed murder of the beautiful, passionately loving Duchess of Praslin by her husband, the Duke, is a story that might well have inspired Browning to write one of his great poems, or might have moved George Meredith to find in real life the material for another "Tragic Comedians." For the Duchess of Praslin's only crime in her sombre husband's eyes seems to have been that of loving him too well. There was, it is true, another woman in the case, but not the least strange part of the story is that not even in France, where such things are easily suspected, did any reasonable human being believe that she had done the Duchess any real wrong; the lady who was thus dragged into the awful drama ended her life in the United States as the respected and beloved wife of a prominent citizen of New York.

In addition to this question of jealousy, the case presents special features of extraordinary and romantic interest—the high rank and social position of the Duke, the painfully moving letters written by the Duchess, the weird incident of the fancy-dress costume, and finally the death of the Duke himself by poison.

I hesitated for some time before including the famous case of Madeleine Smith in this volume; but I felt it would be a mistake to omit it because, though it is vaguely familiar to all those interested in crime, only very compressed accounts of it have been published, if we except the admirable volume devoted to a verbatim report of the trial in the " Great Scottish Trials " series. Not only is the story of profound human interest, but it contains features which would seem incredible if they had not been proved to be facts. The greatest legal authority of the day declared that " never in a criminal case were the chances of condemnation and acquittal more nicely balanced "; and for weeks nothing aroused such interest throughout the whole Empire as the fate of this beautiful girl.

Certain details connected with the story might well have made it difficult of discussion in the ordinary Victorian family circle, yet the human interest of it was too strong for the conventions of even that period. All over Scotland gently nurtured girls prayed each night in an agony of supplication that Madeleine Smith might be acquitted of the awful charge brought against her. And when at last the old-time Scottish verdict of " Not Proven " was returned, it was said that never since the days of Mary Queen of Scots had such a scene of tumult been witnessed in Edinburgh.

The La Pommerais affair is distinguished among the usually sordid " insurance murder " cases by the sinister cleverness of its chief actor ; also because it is, as far as I have been able to discover, the only important case in which the murderer persuaded his victim willingly to poison herself. Incidentally the story has the further interest that the accused man was of noble birth, and was just entering upon what promised to be a brilliant professional career. The Empress Eugénie herself interceded to save his life, and to this day certain Parisians believe him to have been innocent.

None of the cases here narrated is of deeper interest than the mystery which still surrounds the death of Mr. Charles Bravo, about which singularly little has been written or published. This is the more curious as it raises the familiar question—should a woman tell? Must she reveal the fact that, before she met the man whom she now loves and who is about to marry her, she was unfaithful to their joint future? And if the stern moralist, faced with such a problem, answers "Yes" in the case of a girl, would he be equally hard, equally unyielding, if the woman betrothed be a widow?

This case of conscience probes the very quick of human nature. The fact that the beautiful widow, Florence Ricardo, repenting of the past and hoping for a cloudless future, decided to act as most straightforward, and we may add un-tempted, people would have advised her to act, undoubtedly played a decisive part in the still impenetrable mystery of her second husband's death.

Among murder trials of comparatively recent years, one which presented several unusual features was that of the Marquis de Nayve. It illustrates the fact that in each social circle of every civilized community there is ever in being a terrible secret tragedy—the tragedy of the unwanted child. Moralists and philanthropists are well aware that when you probe into the lives of unfortunates of either sex you often find that they were born illegitimate, that is, beyond the law, deprived of the normal tenderness, love, and care which the humblest child is supposed to have a right to enjoy from its birth. It was the existence of an unwanted child which led to the strange and painful mystery which is still in a sense unsolved.

The Chambige affair has been chosen as a supreme type of the French *crime passionel.* It was the mysterious element in this tragic story which aroused such fierce feelings of partizanship that all over France there were households where the subject had to be banned—the women, with scarce an exception, taking the part of their fellow-woman, the men the part of their fellow-man.

In this, more than in almost any case of the kind, the student of human nature is confronted with a mystery which lies deep within the roots of humanity, those roots from which spring the upas trees of passion, of hate, of jealousy, of fear. The facts seem to support each of the two possible explanations in turn. The writer confesses that he himself finds it impossible to make up his mind as to where the truth lies.

Henri Chambige, the melancholy hero of the story, was once tutor to the sons of the French novelist who is famous under the pseudonym of

"Gyp." She formed a very strong opinion as to what really took place, and she wrote a remarkable story, " Un Raté," in which she used to some extent the known facts of the case.

It is strange that the Peltzer affair should have attracted so little attention in England at the time it took place, and yet it may be doubted if there has ever been in the history of crime a more extraordinary and dramatic story. It owes its intense human interest to the fact that the plot, of which the motive was an absorbing and yet unconfessed passion for a noble and high-minded woman, was conceived and carried out with real intellectual ability by the man who, if he did not actually commit, undoubtedly inspired, the murder.

Never was a crime executed with greater patience and organizing skill; and here we find what is very rare in those murder mysteries which have become widely known to the world, that is, a powerful alliance of time, money, and brains, all used to divert suspicion from the right clue and to cover every incriminating trace. For a considerable period the two criminals felt sure they had succeeded—that the manner in which William Bernays had met his death would always be considered an unfortunate accident.

Everything had been thought out beforehand—
everything, that is, except one apparently trivial
point about the writing of a letter, on which the
organizer of the plot had failed to give proper
instructions to his subordinate. But that one
little slip was enough to give the police the clue,
and it led inevitably to the remorseless tearing
asunder of the whole complicated web of decep-
tion which had been woven with such extra-
ordinarily patient skill and cunning. If the two
men had been equally intelligent, equally able,
it is certain that this most extraordinary murder
would never have been discovered.

The reflection is inevitable that, since in so
many of these cases the discovery of the crime
has depended upon a mere accident, there must
be many others in which the criminals have been
more fortunate and have therefore escaped.
The proportion which the undetected crimes
bear to the detected will always be a matter of
dispute. I am inclined to think that the proportion is not so large as timid people often
imagine, and that the majority of murders and
attempted murders which are undetected are
cases of poisoning.

I once asked a very wise old family physician
for his opinion on this point. He replied that,
while he had had his suspicions in more cases

than he could remember, he had only felt certain of seven cases in all his long years of practice. By that he did not of course mean that his certainty necessarily amounted in any of the seven instances to legal certainty, justifying him in denouncing any person as a secret poisoner.

Everyone will remember the ludicrous disgust of the first murderer who was caught by means of the electric telegraph. He felt a genuine grievance that the arm of the law had not played fair! Since that case, while the progress of science and invention has furnished the criminal with new and powerful weapons, it has been probably of even greater service to the detection of crime. Some of the mysteries narrated in these pages would certainly have been solved if the scientific knowledge available had been what it is now. Moreover, there can be no doubt that modern chemical and biological research is steadily reducing the risk of judicial error, more especially in cases of suspected poisoning.

I
THE STRANGE CASE OF MARIE LAFARGE

THE STRANGE CASE OF MARIE LAFARGE

I

WE are peeping into one of those long, straight corridors which are to be found in almost all old French country houses. Down one side is a row of high, narrow windows looking into a gloomy and thickly-wooded park; down the other side are ranged in a long, regular line, the doors to the best bedrooms of the Château des Glandiers.

Charles Lafarge and his Parisian bride arrived here only an hour ago, and a number of Charles's relatives and friends are waiting downstairs to greet and welcome the new mistress of Les Glandiers.

The visitors are growing rather impatient, for young Madame Lafarge went upstairs to change her travelling dress within a few minutes of her arrival, and she has not yet reappeared, although she must be aware that, in this part of France at any rate, folk remain faithful to old custom and dine at six o'clock. Fortunately, the bride-

3

groom's mother and sister are there to entertain
the company.

The bridegroom himself—a good-looking young
man of only eight-and-twenty—is pacing up and
down the corridor with long, impatient steps.
Every now and again he stops before one of the
closed doors, turns the handle, and, finding that
it does not yield, shakes it violently.

" Marie ! " he calls out angrily.   " Marie !
Open the door !   What do you mean by locking
yourself in like this ?   Understand that I am
your husband, and that I have the right to order
you to open the door ! "

Then he takes another turn up and down the
corridor.   Again he approaches the closed door,
and in a changed and pleading voice he whispers,
" Marie ! Do open to me ! My mother and
sister, to say nothing of the others, cannot make
out what is going on.   Surely you cannot mean
to lock me out of our room—me, your loving,
your devoted Charles ? "

But still there comes no answer from behind
the locked door.   The unfortunate young husband, however, soon hears the murmur of two
voices—he knows them to be those of his young
wife and of the lady's maid, her foster-sister, who
accompanied them from Paris on the honeymoon.

Once more Charles begins pacing up and
down.   He feels absolutely at his wits' end.

Suddenly, to his secret relief, there appears at
the head of the staircase at the end of the long
corridor a determined-looking elderly lady whom
he dearly loves and respects, for she is his mother,
Madame Lafarge mère.

"Well?" she says briefly. "Well, Charles,
what does all this mean?"

"I'm sure I don't know, mother," he falters
out. "I suppose poor Marie is tired—tired and
excited."

"That is all very well, my son, but Marie
must really make an effort. Everyone downstairs, not only our relations, but the neighbours
who have come to greet her, are more amazed
than I can tell you."

Madame Lafarge looks angrily, though at the
same time tenderly, at her son, and, turning on
her heel, goes slowly downstairs again.

Once more Charles approaches the locked door
and rattles the handle.

"Marie!" he whispers urgently. "Do you
realise how great a shame and affront you are
putting on me? For heaven's sake, come out
and behave like a reasonable woman!"

And then, to his immeasurable relief, he sees
an envelope being pushed under the door.

Eagerly he stoops and takes it up. And then,
as his eyes glance down the first few lines of the
first letter his wife has ever written to him—for
Marie is a French girl, and during their brief

engagement had no occasion to write to her lover
—Charles Lafarge utters a hoarse cry, and in-
stinctively retreats into one of the shallow
embrasures of the corridor windows.

Charles: [So began the extraordinary
letter which was destined to produce a
most unhappy effect at the trial of Marie
Lafarge]

I do not blame you! I do not wish to
say anything against you. All I beg you
to do is to allow me to leave you. Our
marriage has been a terrible mistake. I
take all the blame of it on myself. Nay,
more—I here and now make you a shameful confession.

Pity me, Charles—I love another man!
And this man, my lover, has followed us
during the whole of our wedding journey.
Oh, Charles, forgive me—but I have seen
him, I have had secret meetings with my
love. I used to creep out when you were
asleep. I am ashamed, deeply ashamed, of
my wickedness.

But, Charles, you cannot, knowing this,
wish me to stay with you. I do not ask to
have back my fortune. I only ask you
to let me go away. I will sign any document you like, and I swear I will never
trouble you again.

Oh, Charles, on my knees I implore you
to be merciful and to grant my prayer!
Forget the miserable Marie who has treated
you so ill!

Lafarge's first impulse, on reading this amazing epistle, is to batter in the bedroom door and kill the girl to whose keeping only four days ago he entrusted his honour.

To the vexation and anger he felt at Marie's unreasonable behaviour in thus hiding herself in her bedroom, are now suddenly added the bitter pangs of jealousy; for he adores the beautiful young creature who has just made him this extraordinary and shameful confession.

But he remembers that the house is full of relations and neighbours, and he thrusts away the murderous impulse. Quietly he goes downstairs, takes his mother aside, and shows her his wife's fateful letter.

Now, old Madame Lafarge, though she is already violently prejudiced against her Parisian daughter-in-law, is full of that mingled shrewd sense and feeling of self-respect that is one of the foundations of the French character.

To her son's great surprise, a smile comes over her face.

" Not a word of this is true ! " she exclaims, shaking her head. " Your wife has invented this absurd story, Charles, in order to frighten you, and in order that you may leave her alone. No doubt she does want to go away, back to her family—back to gay Paris. But as to her having a lover—as to his having followed you through the honeymoon, if all you tell me of your honeymoon is true, that is simply untrue—untrue, my son! Allow me to deal with her. I will go upstairs with our two old friends, your uncle and your godfather, and we shall soon see whether we can't bring her to reason."

And Charles Lafarge, with a hopeless gesture, consents.

He would give everything he has in the world to be able to believe his mother's theory of Marie's extraordinary letter.

The old lady, accompanied by the two middle-aged country gentlemen whom she has called to her help in this crisis, come upstairs and join the waiting husband. And then there begins, through the locked door of the bedroom, the kind of negotiation and discussion which is inevitable when a violent family quarrel is going on.

At last the door is opened by the lady's maid, and old Madame Lafarge and her two companions edge their way into a large, gloomy bed-chamber, which is not, it must be admitted, at all the sort of room which a charming young bride would naturally expect to have allotted to her.

Perhaps the two gentlemen feel this. In any case they gaze very kindly at the beautiful young woman who stands before them with tears streaming down her cheeks.

"Marie!" says her mother-in-law gently, much in the tone that one would use in approaching a

timid young animal that one wished to tame.
" Marie! Is it possible that you wrote this
cruel, this mad, this foolish letter to my poor
son Charles ? "

Marie, with a quick, convulsive breath, nods
her head.

" Well, my dear child, you did a very unkind
thing by one who adores you. But for me,
Charles was going out into the park, and by this
time he would have drowned himself in the lake !
He loves you, Marie. Do you not know that he
loves you ? "

Again Marie nods her head, and fresh tears
come into her eyes, for she is warm-hearted and
impulsive.

" I know," says Madame Lafarge impressively,
" I *know* that what you have written in this mad
letter is not true. Confess, my child, that you
made up this absurd story about your having a
lover in order to kill Charles's love for you and
because you want him to allow you to go back to
Paris ! I see that you do not like Les Glandiers;
the place is not like what you expected ; and—
yes, why should I not say it ?—you do not like
the thought of having to live with me and with
your sister-in-law. But, Marie, you need not be
afraid of me ! I am devoted to Charles, and
rather than sacrifice my son's happiness, I would
willingly go and live elsewhere. All I ask you
to do is to *try* and live with me."

The old lady's voice breaks, and Marie begins to feel bitterly ashamed of herself.

Madame Lafarge begins again in those gentle, level tones which seem to make her arguments still more rational and convincing.

" I want to tell you that we are far better off than we appear to be, living in this quiet way in our old house. Only stay and behave like a reasonable woman, and you shall have as much money as you think necessary to make the house pretty and comfortable. To my old eyes, Les Glandiers is perfect as it is, but Charles tells me you are very disappointed—that you have already told him that you think the château ugly and badly furnished."

Poor Marie again feels overwhelmed with shame. Madame Lafarge is talking in such a kind, sensible, dignified way.

The girl-wife hides her face in her hands.

" Confess," says Madame Lafarge persuasively, "confess that you invented all that there is in this letter, and that you have never had a lover either before your marriage or since."

And Marie bends her head.

Charles's godfather, who does not take the whole business as tragically as Charles's mother and uncle seem to do, bursts out laughing.

"Oh, naughty girl!" he exclaims, and an answering smile quivers over Marie's lovely face —"do you mean that you simply made up this story in order to go back to Paris and be neither maid, wife, nor widow?"

Again Marie bends her head.

"Well, well," says the mother. "We won't say anything more about it! Come downstairs at any rate, Marie, and I will manage Charles— I will see that he does not worry you."

They all four go downstairs, and Marie becomes transformed from a savagely determined, hysterical young woman to a gentle, well-conducted bride.

II

It is now time to explain who and what were the newly-married pair who had so extraordinary a home-coming, and into whose intimate private life the public of that day, not only in France, but also in England and Germany, were soon to be suddenly and dramatically admitted.

The cherished younger daughter of Colonel Cappelle, of the Old Guard, one of the great Napoleon's favourite officers, the woman who lives in the criminal annals of France as Marie Lafarge, might, but for her father's premature death, have survived in history among those beautiful and delightful French women who played a great part in the social life of their time.

Through her mother she was, as we have said, granddaughter by Madame de Genlis of that

2

Duke of Orleans who lives in history under the shameful nickname of Philippe Égalité. The fact was well known in Paris society at the time of her marriage.

Most unfortunately for Marie Cappelle, her father died when she was a child, and her mother married again. She was then adopted by her aunt, Madame Garat, whose husband held the important position of Governor of the Bank of France.

Her aunt was very kind to her, and proud of her, but, even so, Marie had a lonely girlhood, and I must dwell on that fact because her one intimate girl friend was destined to play a terrible and fatal part in her short after-life.

This friend, Mademoiselle de Nicolai, belonged to the great French nobility ; Marie's aunt encouraged in every way her niece's friendship, and in those halcyon days of early girlhood the two Maries were inseparable, and loved each other as sisters love.

Strange to say (when we remember the way French girls are brought up, especially girls of position and refinement), Marie Cappelle and her friend were allowed to go to church alone together, and, human nature being much the same in France as it is elsewhere, the two young ladies managed to start a kind of childish flirtation with a young man whom they first met in church, and who was of half-Spanish birth.

According to Marie Cappelle's later account, this man, Flavé by name, was never in love with her at all, but was desperately in love with her friend, Marie de Nicolai; and Marie Cappelle played, as so many girls in such a case have played in the past and will play in the future, the thankless and dangerous part of go-between. She allowed young Flavé to send letters to Mademoiselle de Nicolai under cover to her.

Nothing, however, came of the imprudent flirtation. Flavé never even compassed an introduction to the lady of his dreams. Indeed, within a very few months of the foolish episode, Mademoiselle de Nicolai, being then nineteen, married the Marquis de Liautaud, a Frenchman of high rank and great wealth. As to young Flavé, if the friends ever thought of him at all, he must have remained in their minds as the hero of an affair of which they were both rather ashamed. Neither girl had ever seen him alone —so Madame de Liautaud always solemnly swore till the day of her death.

Be that as it may, Marie Cappelle, more lonely than ever, now that her one intimate friend was married, went on living quietly with her aunt, Madame Garat, in Paris. Several young men fell in love with her and made her offers of marriage, for she was not only exceptionally attractive, but had a dowry of a hundred thousand francs. She was, however, as we know, romantic, and unwilling to make a *mariage de convenance*.

She had reached the age of twenty-three when her uncle one day sent for her to come into his study. There he told her that he had heard of a young country gentleman who had come to Paris to seek a wife, and who, if all that was said of him was true, would make an ideal husband. He added that the name of this possible suitor was Charles Lafarge.

Lafarge was twenty-eight, a member of an honourable provincial family, and an ironmaster in a fair way of business. Also, he owned a delightful country house—a château, in fact—named Les Glandiers, in that beautiful district of France called Le Corrèze. The young man expressed himself as desirous of finding a clever, cultivated wife who would share the rather lonely life he was compelled to lead for the greater part of each year.

Marie, attracted by this account, at last consented to an informal interview with the ironmaster, and it is on record that Charles Lafarge fell in love at first sight with the intelligent, handsome, and accomplished Parisian girl.

On her side, Marie seems to have thought him very plain, and to have found his manners lacking in the grace and refinement to which she was accustomed in the men about her. But Lafarge showed clearly how greatly he was attracted by her, and her family were delighted with the excellent accounts they received of him from all sorts of people—for in France they have the sensible custom of obtaining information about a suitor's character and disposition from those who know him best.   The result was that Marie was soon won over to the view that Charles Lafarge concealed a heart of gold beneath his rough exterior, and that his love would soon bring forth hers.

Mademoiselle Cappelle was informed that she would have to spend a portion of her married life with her mother-in-law and her husband's married sister.   But that fact did not annoy or frighten her as it might have done an English girl, for in provincial France it is usual for the older and the younger people in a family to live together, for at any rate part of each year, in the same house, and, on the whole, the plan generally works very well.

Marie's wedding was attended by many persons of importance in Paris, and it was characteristic of the bride that she spent some money her uncle had given her as a wedding present in gifts to friends she was leaving behind her.

Immediately after the ceremony the young people started homeward on a short honeymoon.

What happened during those first fateful days of married life?—days which may make or mar a woman's subsequent relationship to her husband. According to the account Marie gave afterwards, Charles Lafarge, without being unkind, became at once a very different man as husband from that he had been as lover.

At no time had the ironmaster impressed those about him as particularly refined or gentle-mannered ; and now, when he was sure of his beautiful young wife, he showed himself in his real colours—that is, as a rough and rather boorish individual, determined to have his own way in everything.

Still, Marie never accused him of active unkindness ; she only said that during her honeymoon her eyes were opened to the fact that she had married a man very unlike her-self, one who cared nothing for books, for music, for society, or for anything except business.

The high-strung, romantic girl also found Les Glandiers, her future home, entirely different from what she and her family had been led to believe.

Les Glandiers was not a château in the usual sense of the term. It was a straggling, ugly, dark, damp old house, embowered in trees, and differing in almost every particular, as to its interior arrangements, from what had been described by its owner.

The knowledge that her husband had deceived her in such a foolish and mean way produced on Marie an extraordinary effect. In the light of modern medical science, we may fairly suppose that Charles Lafarge's unhappy bride became violently hysterical; for, after having been greeted, as she imagined, coldly and jealously by Charles's mother and sister, Marie ran upstairs and locked herself in the gloomy bedroom which she was told was to be hers and her husband's.

And then there took place the extraordinary episode which I have tried to reconstitute in all its curious detail.

It is impossible now to tell with certainty what really happened after that strange scene, for each of those who afterwards testified at the trial told a different tale.

But there can be no doubt that Marie Lafarge, thanks to her mother-in-law's diplomacy and good sense, did have a real reconciliation with her husband, and that she persuaded him quite easily to believe that, in very truth, she had never had a lover in the guarded, happy girl-life she had led in Paris as an inmate of her aunt's house.

And she did not carry out the reconciliation in any half-hearted fashion. She made friends with her husband's workmen; she entertained his old neighbours and friends; and she seems also to have tried to make herself pleasant to her mother-in-law. This was her hardest task, for old Madame Lafarge soon became intensely jealous of her only son's love for his wife, and she interfered as much as she dared between the two young people.

By Charles's wish, his mother gave up the management of the house and of the servants into the hands of her daughter-in-law, and this not unnaturally irritated the older lady very much, the more so that Marie's ideas of house-keeping and those of Madame Lafarge mère were very different.

Marie liked everything to be done in a simple yet civilized manner. She had a great dislike to the long, elaborate banquets in which the country folk of France then, as now, delighted, and which consist of from fourteen to twenty courses rather roughly dished up and served, while the guests often stay at table three, four, even five hours! Madame Charles Lafarge insisted that the table-cloth in her dining-room should always be spotlessly clean, and she made the cook understand that the menu, if comparatively short, should consist of food daintily and prettily served.

As to the delicate and all-important question of Marie's relations with her husband, most people will agree that a man does not remain fondly attached to his wife, and eager to fulfil her slightest wish, if she, on her side, goes on being cold and disagreeable to him. Such behaviour on a husband's part may be found in poems and novels, but it does not occur in real life.

Charles Lafarge was evidently a hot-tempered man, and he had little control over his tongue ; and yet, as the weeks and the months rolled by, he became more and more devoted to his wife. Whenever Charles went away on business for two or three days, he wrote Marie adoring letters, and, as we have seen, though he was as truly attached to his mother as are all good Frenchmen, he gave his wife power over everything in the household, including those which his mother considered ought still to have lain in her province.

From the point of view of their neighbours and friends, the Charles Lafarges were a model couple, and, thanks to Marie's efforts, Les Glandiers soon became a very pleasant and agreeable country house.

III

At last there came a day when the husband and wife agreed that Lafarge should go to Paris in order to raise money to develop a new patent in connection with his ironworks. But he did not inform either Marie or his mother of the fact that his finances had already become greatly

2*

involved, and that, apart altogether from the patent, it was essential to him to procure a loan.

Now, it might be thought that Marie would have been eager to take this opportunity of going back to her early home and seeing her relations and the friends of her girlhood. But she suggested nothing of the kind ; in fact, she behaved with great good sense.

" You wiłł be doing a good deal of tiring and worrying business," she said, " and I had much better stay here, and look after the house and the different things that we are having done to improve the place. Go you up alone to Paris, dear Charles, and I will do everything in my power to help you by giving you introductions to business friends of my family."

Much to Marie's annoyance and surprise, Lafarge insisted on taking with him his foreman, a man named Denis, who had a great deal of influence over him, and with whom he had already had secret money dealings of a very shady kind—though, of· course, Marie was quite unaware of them.

That this man played a great part in the drama which was soon to follow no one can doubt, and, according to two eminent German lawyers who wrote a book on the Lafarge case, it was Denis, not Marie, who ought ultimately to have stood in the dock.

Just before Lafarge and his foreman started for Paris, Marie fell ill, and her husband nursed her in the most devoted manner. One day, when she was getting better, she suddenly told Charles that she had been so deeply touched by his love and care of her that she had made her will, leaving him the sole use of her fortune during his lifetime, though, if she and Charles had no child, the money was to go ultimately to her own nephews and nieces. Lafarge, much moved by this proof of his wife's love, also made his will, leaving Marie everything he possessed.

Now, it is a curious fact that Marie Lafarge at once sent off Charles's will to a local lawyer, although she left her own will in the house. This was a strange thing for her to do, but she afterwards pointed out that she had a good reason for it, as her mother-in-law and sister-in-law were always searching among her papers and showing the most indiscreet curiosity as to the contents of any letters she received.

At last Charles Lafarge went off to Paris; and at once there began the most tender correspondence between the husband and wife. Marie had an unusual literary gift, and in her letters she drew, in moving language, a description of her loneliness and her longing for his return. Charles, on his side, also wrote very affectionate letters, telling her—or so she believed—every detail of the difficult business which had brought him to Paris. As an actual fact he did not tell her very much, and he and Denis engaged in many peculiar money transactions which only came to light long afterwards.

The ironmaster had been away rather more than a month when a curious incident took place. It was one which later made a very strong and sinister impression on the public, as well as on Marie's judge and jury.

Les Glandiers seems to have been infested with rats, as are so many old country houses, and Marie Lafarge commissioned one of her servants to buy some arsenic with a view to ridding the place of the vermin. Now, very shortly after this purchase had been made, she wrote and informed Charles that she was sending him a box containing, in addition to a miniature of herself which had been done by a lady of the neighbourhood, a few home-made cakes.

Madame Lafarge mère was noted for her good cooking, particularly for the making of a certain kind of small cream cake.

Marie further proposed in her letter that Charles should eat one of these cakes at twelve o'clock on a certain night, and she undertook herself to eat a similar cake exactly at the same moment. She added a request that he would not tell anyone about this sentimental refection !

In due course the box arrived in Paris, but Lafarge did not open it himself; instead, he told one of the hotel servants to do so. The servant opened the box, and both this man and Lafarge, who was standing by him as he prised the lid open, noticed that there was only one large cake inside. Lafarge then and there broke off a small piece of the cake, and, observing " My wife sent me this," ate it.

That night he was taken violently ill. This was proved by the hotel books, for on the following day he stayed in bed and had invalid food sent up to him.

The rest of the cake was thrown into a drawer, and some time later—in fact, after Lafarge had left Paris—one of the hotel servants ate a piece of it, and he also was taken ill in exactly the same way as Lafarge had been.

Meanwhile Marie Lafarge—but for this we have only the testimony of the mother-in-law who hated her, and it was testimony given after the poor woman fully believed that her daughter-in-law had poisoned her son—began to show the most surprising uneasiness about her husband's health. She said that she was haunted by a presentiment that she would soon be a widow, and she seemed thoroughly unhappy and miserable.

As to Charles Lafarge, he soon recovered, and the next news received at Les Glandiers was that he was starting for home, accompanied by his foreman, Denis. On the way the two men visited a lawyer, who lent Lafarge a thousand pounds in notes and gold. But this fact was carefully concealed from young Madame Lafarge and from Charles's mother.

We now come to the real drama, to that part of the story which will remain a mystery to the end of time.

Lafarge was very far from well when he arrived at Les Glandiers ; indeed, while expressing the greatest joy at seeing his wife again, he was so unwell that he had to go to bed at once.

Marie herself brought him his supper, which consisted of a cold truffled fowl, and she and he ate it together by his bedside.

No sooner had he finished his meal than Charles was taken terribly ill, with symptoms that were believed later to have been those of poisoning, though at the time no one suspected it. These symptoms were a terrible heat in the throat, horrible gnawing pains in the stomach, and an awful sense of icy coldness.

He also complained very much of the noise the rats still made in the house, and his wife—for the second time—bought arsenic, but on this occasion through the medium of the foreman Denis.

Long, weary days followed at Les Glandiers. Lafarge lay ill, eating very little, living entirely on liquid food, everything which he ate being more or less prepared, and always handed to him, by the devoted Marie, whom he could hardly bear out of his sight.

The history of the illness now becomes complicated by the presence in the house of a new inmate, a middle-aged lady who was an intimate friend of Charles's mother and sister.

This lady, Madame Brun, seems to have been used as a kind of spy by her two friends; she watched the unsuspecting Marie very closely, and she noticed—or declared afterwards that she noticed—that whenever young Madame Lafarge was about to hand her husband anything to drink, she always put into the cup or glass a spoonful of white powder.

Lafarge daily grew worse and worse, and at last his wife became so much alarmed that she begged the local doctor who was attending him to call in another physician in consultation.

It was proved afterwards that Marie Lafarge was really far more eager than was Charles's mother that this should be done, and, further, that she wished the best doctor in the neighbourhood to be called. Old Madame Lafarge objected to this step, apparently because she had once had a quarrel with the doctor in question.

It cannot be stated too clearly that up to that time no one, least of all Lafarge's regular medical attendant, suspected poison. The doctor, indeed, made light of Marie's fears, and told her that Charles Lafarge had been subject to such attacks of sickness and colic from childhood; this fact should be remembered in view of the evidence afterwards tendered at the trial by Marie's deadly enemies.

If the people round Charles Lafarge had any reason to suppose his wife was poisoning him, they were, of course, lacking in the commonest humanity in not immediately doing something to stop the completion of the crime; but, though they all afterwards declared that they had suspected Marie early in the case, we may take it that they did not really do so until a very short time before his death.

What first caused the mother to entertain so awful a suspicion, we shall never know. It may have been a word said by Madame Brun; it may have been an insinuation made by the real murderer—if Marie was innocent; or it may have been some remark made by the doctor.

Be that as it may, old Madame Lafarge suddenly became convinced that her son was being poisoned by his apparently loving and devoted wife.

As to the arsenic which had been bought, at Marie's orders, by the foreman Denis, it was made into a paste—which, strange to say, had no effect on the rats.

And then, for the third time, young Madame Lafarge procured poison from a country town near by. On this occasion she herself wrote a friendly little letter to the chemist, telling him the purpose for which she required it. But it should be added that he was a personal acquaintance ; this, perhaps, was why he sent her a very large quantity of arsenic.

Charles Lafarge grew so much worse that at last, by his wife's wish, and against that of his mother and sister, a new doctor was called in consultation. But old Madame Lafarge chose for this purpose a quite young man, instead of the well-known and authoritative physician whom Marie had desired should be sent for. And to this youthful stranger Charles's mother at once confided her suspicion that Marie was slowly but surely poisoning her unhappy son.

The young doctor seems to have at once accepted this dreadful suggestion as a fact, and that without even attempting to find out whether there was any ground for it or not. Moreover, without telling his colleague of his intention, he decided on what most people will agree was a very wrong and cruel course ; he decided, that is, that it was his duty to tell the now dying man that he was being done to death, and by the wife in whom he implicitly trusted.

Now, how did the unfortunate Lafarge receive this frightful information ? The doctor afterwards asserted that his patient took the news calmly, and told him, as confirmatory evidence, of the illness he had had in Paris after eating the cake that Marie had sent him !

But there is ample evidence that Lafarge, even after the doctor had revealed to him his mother's awful suspicion, behaved to his wife Marie exactly as he had done before—he still spoke to her in terms of adoring affection, he still would not allow her out of his sight, and he still refused to take any food, excepting from her hand.

Against this evidence must be set one opposing statement made by Lafarge's sister, but we shall see how slight and fanciful that statement is compared with the testimony of all the other people who were in the house during those long, mournful days.

The sands of the unhappy man's life were running out very fast, and at last there came the dread moment when the dying man's wife, his mother, and his sister, together with various other relations, came and knelt by his bedside awaiting the end.

Suddenly Lafarge muttered to his sobbing mother : " You hurt me—please go away ! " She was supported out of the room, the others present also left, and there remained with the dying man only his wife and his sister.

What then happened was thus afterwards described by the sister.

Lafarge hoarsely exclaiming, " I want to drink ! " Marie rushed forward with some water. But Lafarge opened his eyes, and—still only according to his sister's evidence—a dreadful smile came over his face as he pushed the glass his wife's hand held out to him from his lips.

It is a rather strange fact that Marie left the room some minutes before her husband's death ; thus she was not present when he actually passed away.

IV

The moment Charles Lafarge was dead, in fact before the breath could have been well out of his poor, tortured body, there took place at Les Glandiers an extraordinary and dramatic scene, and one which must have been carefully planned beforehand.

The young widow was enticed by a trick out of the bedroom where she was lying crying on her bed ; she was persuaded to go into another room, and there the key of the door was turned on her.

Then old Madame Lafarge and her daughter rushed into Marie's room, forced the locks of her boxes and of her cupboards, and began to search, in feverish haste, for some kind of proof that Marie had indeed poisoned Charles.

Although they found nothing, she was kept a prisoner for many hours ; in fact, until her mother-in-law and the doctor had informed the nearest magistrate of their suspicions.

The magistrate hurried to Les Glandiers, and took Marie's guilt for granted before any proof of it had been laid before him. Indeed, the wretched, bewildered young woman found herself accused, and practically condemned as a murderess of a peculiarly cold-blooded and wicked type, before she had been able to gather her wits together, and before she had been allowed to communicate with her family in Paris.

Meanwhile the two doctors were holding a rough post-mortem examination of the corpse, and the result was a great surprise. They were both compelled to admit that they had not been able to discover any trace of poison in Lafarge's body.

The result of this examination seems to have shaken even old Madame Lafarge's belief in her daughter-in-law's guilt. She came and humbly begged Marie's pardon for having suspected her, and Marie, in the very curious autobiography which she wrote while in prison awaiting her trial, declares that she did forgive old Madame Lafarge, and that she even promised to remain on at Les Glandiers and be a daughter to her.

Marie, now quite reassured, sat down and wrote to her relations. But she only informed them of Charles's death; and she also, however, asked them to send her a good lawyer from Paris, as she had reason to fear, by certain things which had been said when Lafarge was dying, that his money matters were in a very serious state.

From this letter it is clear that Marie gave very little thought to the terrible accusation which had been levelled at her. She was only four-and-twenty, accustomed to receive homage and love from all those about her, and old Madame Lafarge's suspicions probably seemed to her—if she was indeed innocent—to be caused by the old lady's jealous grief.

But the judicial authorities had not been satisfied with the post-mortem, and they ordered a further and much more thorough investigation.

One evening, as Marie was sitting alone in her drawing-room, a gentleman of the neighbourhood, who was evidently attracted by her beauty and loneliness, came in and, with some agitation, told her that if she were wise she would flee the country.

" I have a carriage and a good pair of horses close by," he said. " I have also a passport which I have procured as for my wife, and which will do very well for you. I implore you most earnestly to leave France without waiting for the result of the inquiry they are about to hold into this matter of your husband's death. Re-

member that a great lawyer once declared, ' If
I were accused of stealing the towers of Notre-
Dame I should hurry off without waiting to be
arrested ! ' ”

This suggestion seems to have been rejected
with indignation by Marie Lafarge. She told
her kind neighbour that she was not in the least
afraid, and that, being quite innocent, she had
no reason to fear that she would ever be troubled
again.

Meanwhile, the police had been making all
sorts of inquiries about the dead man, his past
relations with his wife, and so on ; but, without
waiting for more evidence, the same magistrate
who had come before, on the day of Charles's
death, came again to Les Glandiers, and, to
Marie's surprise and indignation, subjected her
to a close and pitiless interrogation.

Everyone who had been in the house at the
time of the death—Madame Brun, who gave
fateful testimony against her ; the foreman
Denis, who seems to have always hated her ;
her maid and foster-sister, who with tears and
anger eagerly asserted her mistress's innocence ;
her mother-in-law, who was now once more
quite convinced that Marie had poisoned Charles
—all were examined and cross-examined at
immense length.

Marie's own examination lasted three hours,
and at the end of it the magistrate made up his

mind that she had indeed poisoned her husband, though no motive, save that of personal dislike, could be suggested.

The warrant for her arrest was signed, but Marie was allowed to take her maid with her to the prison, and drive there in her own carriage.

V

On her arrival at Brives, the pretty little town where the second act of the drama was to take place, Marie Lafarge had to face a terrible ordeal, for the whole population had turned out to hoot the beautiful young woman who was already, in local estimation, condemned as a cruel and treacherous poisoner.

Meanwhile, Marie's family, all those well-known, well-placed, important people in Paris who loved and admired her, had received the news of her arrest with shocked incredulity. It was inconceivable to them that the delightful, beautiful girl of whom they had been so proud, and at whose marriage they had been present less than a year before, was actually lying in prison under a shameful accusation of murder.

They acted with promptitude, courage, and good feeling. Without losing any time, they engaged a famous Paris barrister to prepare her defence ; but, unfortunately, they went to one who was really too busy to give up his work in the capital to defend a prisoner, however important, in a far-off corner of provincial France.

It was then that Marie Lafarge suddenly bethought herself that she had met, during the early days of her married life, a very remarkable young advocate, a man of only two-and-twenty, named Lachaud. She wrote him the following pathetic, if rather affected, little letter :

> THE PRISON, BRIVES.
>
> *Monsieur,*
>
> When I was still happy, careless, gay, I heard you defend a poor woman accused of theft, and your words brought tears to my eyes. Now that I am wretched, careworn, and sad, I call on you to help me. I am suffering from the burden of an awful, and a false, accusation. Make me smile again, and fill with light the eyes that have wept so many bitter tears during the last few days.

Lachaud, ardent, romantic, generous-hearted, at once responded to this appeal. He came to Brives without a moment's delay, and henceforth this man, who was to become the greatest French advocate of his time, and to attain a position analogous to that of " silver-tongued " Coleridge, or rather that of Sir Charles Russell in England, remained firmly convinced of Marie Lafarge's innocence.

Nay, more ; there is very little doubt that soon

a great tenderness filled Lachaud's heart for the
fascinating Marie. The world has never been
given his half of the correspondence, but many
of her letters to him have been published ; they
are most moving, and prove how close the tie
between them was soon to become.

There can be little doubt that, had Lachaud
secured her acquittal, he would have married
Marie Lafarge. As it was, he worked for her
as no lawyer ever worked before for a client.
And no lawyer ever had a harder task.

For now, like a bolt from the blue, a new
accusation fell on the already burdened shoulders
of the unhappy Marie.

She had not been in prison more than a few
days, and Lachaud had come into the case only
a few hours, when the Public Prosecutor received
a letter signed " Marquis de Liautaud." In it
the writer begged that a special search might be
instituted at Les Glandiers, as he had reason to
believe that a valuable set of diamonds belonging
to his wife—who, as Mademoiselle de Nicolai,
had been Marie's greatest friend—had been
stolen by young Madame Lafarge during a visit
she had paid to his wife and himself shortly after
their marriage.

This accusation seemed to Lachaud, as also
to Marie's relations, so ridiculous and so far-
fetched that they did not at first tell her it had

been made. But a search was instituted at Les
Glandiers, and the diamonds in question were
found in Marie Lafarge's dressing-case !

Feeling something very like despair and horror
—perhaps, if all the truth were known, with
their belief in her innocence a good deal shaken—
they went and told the prisoner of the accusation
and of the discovery. To their amazement and
relief, Marie did not seem in the least surprised
or even ashamed.

"Oh, that's all right !" she exclaimed, something like a smile for the first time illuminating
her now worn, though still beautiful, face. "The
Marquise de Liautaud knows all about it, and
she will certainly see me righted. It is very
wrong of her husband to have written to the
Public Prosecutor without telling her what he
was about to do."

"But surely," cried Lachaud, "you can tell
me the truth without waiting for your friend's
explanation ? "

"No," she said firmly, "I cannot tell even
you, my kind, generous defender; for this
business of the diamonds is a secret between
her and me. All I can do is to give you a
letter to my friend begging her to tell you the
truth."

Nothing could move her from this resolute
attitude, and at last Lachaud reluctantly started
off for Paris—a much longer journey then than

it is now—and sought out the young married
lady who had been Marie Lafarge's almost
sister in the days when they were girls together.
The Marquise de Liautaud was not at all
anxious to meet her one-time friend's lawyer.
But Lachaud was a determined man, and he
made his way into her presence and forced
her to read Marie's pathetic appeal to her to
tell the truth as to the mystery of the diamonds.

We can imagine, as shortly after all France
imagined, the dramatic scene.

The young provincial lawyer, still quite unknown, but full of the intellectual power and
great practical ability which are to make him
the greatest advocate of his time, at last stands
face to face with the Marquise.

It is a duel between these two. Lachaud is
determined to make Madame de Liautaud say
to him that which will clear his beautiful client,
with whom he is already deeply in love, from a
shameful accusation—an accusation even more
shameful, in a sense, than that under which she
lay when first arrested.

" I implore you, Madame, to tell the truth,
even if it costs you a little humiliation ! "

" I do not quite know what you want me to
say," she answers slowly, handing him back
Marie Lafarge's letter. " I do not understand
what poor Marie means by the ' mystery,'

Monsieur. For there is no mystery. My diamonds disappeared, and, though I did not suspect my friend, my husband and his family were always convinced that Marie had taken them. As for me, I thought they had been stolen by a servant."

Even now we cannot tell whether the Marquise de Liautaud told the truth, the half-truth, or a positive lie in that momentous interview with Lachaud. But she certainly came out victorious in the struggle of wills—and, beside himself with disappointment, fear, and anger, Lachaud rushed back with his bad news to Brives.

Then, and even then most reluctantly, Marie Lafarge consented to tell him her version of the diamond mystery.

It was a simple story, and on the face of it supported by certain letters she was able to produce. These letters which Marie Lafarge showed Lachaud were Félix Flavé's old love letters, written when Marie was playing the foolish, perilous part of go-between in a love affair which ought never to have begun.

According to Marie Lafarge the affair had not ended with those few silly sentimental letters. Flavé—now, it seems, settled in Algiers—had tried to blackmail Madame de Liautaud, and it was in order to buy off the lover of her girlhood that the Marquise had entrusted her diamonds to her friend, with the understanding that Marie was to sell them as soon as she could manage it, and transmit the proceeds to the blackmailer.

In our time the truth as to Flavé and his relations to the Marquise de Liautaud would have been dragged into the full light of day, and that even if the trial of Marie Lafarge had had to be postponed for weeks or months. But in spite of Lachaud's frantic efforts to compel Flavé's presence at the trial, the young man was allowed to remain in Algiers, and no attempt was made to force him to give evidence.

As for the Marquise, she declared on oath that Flavé's love—if love it could be called— had been bestowed on Marie Cappelle and not on herself.

This comparatively unimportant question of the Marquise's diamonds proved a crucial point in the trial of Marie Lafarge for murder. Although it was, of course, clear that Marie might be a thief without being a murderer, many people took the view that if she was capable of lying about the one matter, then she was capable also of having contrived and carried out the darker crime.

All France, and especially all French society, began vehemently and passionately to take " sides," indeed, practically the whole nation might have been divided into "Lafargists" and "Anti-Lafargists." The Marquise de Liautaud was also a beautiful and attractive young woman with many attached friends and innumerable relations in the great nobility. These naturally all took her part, and declared her incapable of having indulged in a vulgar flirtation. They pointed triumphantly to the fact that Marie Lafarge could not show a single letter in which the Marquise, in the days when she was Marie Nicolai, mentioned Flavé by name, or even alluded to him.

To the indignation and distress of Madame Lafarge's friends and supporters, the accusation of theft was taken first, and formed a separate case.

Once more was fought a duel, but this time with the buttons off the foils, and between two women. The Marquise was fighting for her reputation—Marie for her life.

Lachaud, after taking counsel with various great pundits of the law, decided to allow judgment, in that first trial, to go by default.

So Marie Lafarge, though she was compelled to be present in the dock, refused to go into the box, though the Marquise de Liautaud, supported by the presence of her husband, her father, and her brothers, of course did so.

Dressed in widow's weeds, Marie Lafarge, pale, trembling, and with tears welling up in her large blue eyes, stood in the dock while her one-time dearest friend swore that, to the best of her reluctant belief, the prisoner had not only stolen her jewels, but had also built up an elaborate and shâmeful story to account for having them in her possession.

The first round was lost by Marie Lafarge, for she was declared guilty of the theft and condemned to two years' imprisonment.

Lachaud gave notice of appeal, and there were no fewer than three trials held in connection with the diamond mystery.

Meanwhile public opinion was being roused, not in France alone, but all over the Continent of Europe. In Brives itself and in the neighbourhood of Les Glandiers the tide had turned with dramatic suddenness in Marie's favour. She received in her prison over six thousand letters of sympathy, and to each of these letters she is said to have sent an eloquent and moving answer.

Though in far from good health, she was always ready to submit to the endless examinations and cross-examinations which form an integral part of the French criminal law, and she behaved as the innocent, in the popular imagination, should always behave ; that is, she was indignant, scornful, pleading, and defiant by turns, and never for one moment did she give up hope.

VI

At last, nearly a year after the death of
Charles Lafarge, the trial of Marie Lafarge on
the charge of having poisoned her husband
opened at Tulle, and people journeyed there
from all over Europe to be present, much as
they did many years later to Rennes, to witness
the trial of Captain Dreyfus.

Madame Lafarge was defended by three barristers, and of the three the one who proved
himself their master, by reason of his matchless
eloquence and clear powers of close reasoning,
was the young and still unknown Lachaud,
fighting for the life of the woman he loved.

When Lachaud made his famous speech in
defence of Madame Lafarge he was only twenty-
three, and many of the people in the court must
have been aware of his personal devotion to the
woman who stood in the dock. But what im-
presses the reader of the first of those great
" plaidoiries," which were to be a monument of
enduring fame, is rather the clear, cold logic
than the impassioned eloquence with which his
name was afterwards to be associated. He was
far too truly convinced of his unhappy friend's
innocence to make any specious attempt to move
the hearts of the jury. One feels, as one reads,
that in his eyes Marie Cappelle, as he called her
during the whole speech, was so completely

innocent of the charge against her that it was
impossible the truth should not prevail.

Only once, quite at the end, did he show
emotion :

"Nous portons de la passion dans ce débat,
dit-on ? Eh bien! oui, je ne m'en défends pas !
J'ai une passion profonde pour le malheur que
j'estime ; oui, j'ai trouvé dans ma raison et dans
mon cœur l'innocence de Marie Cappelle, et
plus son infortune est grande plus mon dévoue-
ment sera entier, absolu."

The trial lasted seventeen days, and the
moment it opened it became terribly clear, not
only to Marie Lafarge's three devoted defenders,
but also to the crowd of men and women who
watched the proceedings with breathless interest,
that the prosecution was absolutely convinced of
the prisoner's guilt.   In fact, it may be doubted
whether there has ever been, in any civilized
country, so determined an effort to prove a
prisoner guilty, in the face of favourable evidence,
than that which judged and condemned Marie
Lafarge.

The first question—though it is a question
which had been, curiously enough, put aside and
forgotten in the excitement caused by the affair
of the diamonds—was, of course, whether
Charles Lafarge had really been poisoned at all.

It will be remembered that the two doctors
who had attended the dead man had held a

3

rough post-mortem examination, which, to their surprise, yielded no result. And now, for the second time, the remains of Lafarge were handed over to two more doctors, Paris scientists of world-wide reputation. The more noted of the two, Dupuytren, declared in the most solemn way that he had not been able to find any trace of arsenic in the body.

This time poor Marie thought herself saved. An extraordinary scene took place in the court-house. The public cheered; Lachaud almost went mad with joy; and Marie fainted from excitement and relief.

But stay—her ordeal was not yet over. The judge coldly ordered that the man who perfected what is still called Marsh's test for the discovery of arsenic should be subpœnaed to make a final examination. His name was Orfila.

Accordingly, Orfila was summoned. Instead, however, of bringing with him two other scientific chemists, as he had been asked to do, he simply brought a young pupil of his own, and it is said that before he made the experiment he observed to a friend: "I am quite sure that I shall find arsenic in Lafarge's body!"

Be that as it may, the Lafarge trial lives in the romantic story of criminal jurisprudence as having been the first in which Marsh's test was applied. The first two tests produced entirely negative results; but on the third test slight traces of arsenic appeared on the testing-plate.

One night elapsed between the making of this test and the publication of the result; and when Madame Lafarge was brought into court, those about her saw that the dark hair, which was one of her chief claims to beauty, had become thickly streaked with grey.

Orfila rose and declared in a funereal voice that he had found arsenic in the remains of the dead man, and he reminded the court that in certain circumstances the over-administration of the poison, while surely killing the victim, leaves but few traces of the drug in the body.

In vain the defence passionately declared that, even if it were proved conclusively that Lafarge had been poisoned, that did not prove his wife a poisoner. They could not say, what they could have said to-day, that there are traces of arsenic in every human body, but they did point out how terribly embarrassed Lafarge's affairs had become before his death.

Was it not possible that he had poisoned himself? They also asked what had become of the thousand pounds which he had received on his way back from Paris, and which had disappeared on the day of his death. Was it not possible that whoever had stolen that sum—for it was never found, though careful search was made for it—had poisoned Lafarge?

We now know that the defence were convinced that the foreman Denis, who, after giving cruel witness against his late mistress, had left his home for ever, was the real criminal.

The last scene of the trial was most impressive. Marie Lafarge was solemnly condemned, not only to death, but also to that barbarous old punishment, which had not then been abolished in France, known as the " Exposition "—in other words, the pillory.

But the dread sentence so far left the prisoner undismayed that she rose in the dock and in a firm voice uttered the words : " Gentlemen, I am innocent ! "

VII

Protests poured in to the Government from all over France. It was whispered that, were an attempt made to guillotine Madame Lafarge, a rescue would be organized, in which thousands of men and women belonging to every class of the community would take part.

This, perhaps, was the real reason why Marie Lafarge was spared both the pillory and the guillotine ; for, after some delay, her sentence was commuted to penal servitude for life.

Marie's own friends and her thousands of unknown sympathisers remained very faithful to her throughout her captivity.

Her pathetic charm won over the governor of her prison and her gaolers. She was allowed the great privilege of writing, and she kept up what may truly be described as an enormous correspondence with all sorts of people—men and women, the majority unknown to her—who continued to take an active sympathy in her case. Part of this correspondence has been published quite lately, and it certainly proves her to have inherited her grandmother, Madame de Genlis's, great literary gift. She also wrote, while in prison, her memoirs—a most curious human document—and "The Hours of a Prisoner," a touching little religious work, which was not published until after her death.

After twelve years of patient waiting, during much of which she was in very bad health, she was released, doubtless owing to efforts made by Lachaud, her one-time advocate and lover, who had by then become famous, and a man whom no French Government could afford to despise.

But, when there came the order of release, Marie Lafarge was in no state to profit by her liberty. The world in which she found herself knew her no more. She had become to the men and women of her own generation a shadowy ghost around whom had raged one of the great battles of their youth.

Her relatives took her to a little watering-

place, and there she died some five months after
leaving prison.

It was said that during Madame Lafarge's
imprisonment Denis—that sinister, mysterious
human being who, according to the two German
jurisconsults who wrote a huge book on the case,
was undoubtedly the real murderer—had been
seen haunting the neighbourhood of her prison.

As for Félix Flavé, who with a word could
have cleared up the diamond mystery, he died in
a mad-house the same year that Marie died; but
not before a very curious fact had come to the
knowledge of Maître Lachaud.

It seems that just about the time when,
according to Marie Lafarge, Madame de
Liautaud was being blackmailed by Flavé, a
French official of the same name, also living in
Algiers, received a mysterious box from Paris to
whose sender he had no clue.   On inquiry, however, he learned that the box had been sent to
Algiers by some one named Liautaud, and that
it was intended for a namesake of his, to whom
he forwarded it unopened.

On this information, Lachaud tried to reopen
the case, but, as might have been expected, he
failed to convince the Court of Appeal that the
prisoner's possible innocence of the lesser crime
exonerated her from the greater of which she
had been tried and found guilty.   But the story,

if true, goes far to prove that Marie Lafarge was indeed martyr rather than murderess.

And now comes perhaps the most amazing fact to be stated in connection with this extraordinary story. The case, as has been said, continues to excite interest in European legal circles, and an opinion has grown up among the jurisconsults not only that Marie Lafarge was not guilty, but that Charles Lafarge was not poisoned at all—in fact, that he died a natural death.

This is the view now held by those who make a special study of criminal jurisprudence, and quite recently the writer of this book was assured that this was his view by the leading European authority on the criminal use of arsenic.

Maître Lachaud lived to be a very old man, but he never forgot Marie Lafarge. He paid for the upkeep of her grave for something like forty years; her portrait hung in his study above his writing-table; and to the very end of his long life no subject could rouse him to such eloquent and eager speech as the question of the innocence of the long dead, but still remembered and cherished, woman.

II
CAN A WIFE LOVE TOO WELL?

CAN A WIFE LOVE TOO WELL ?

THE DUCHESS OF PRASLIN

I

THE supposed murder of the beautiful, passionately loving Duchess of Praslin by her husband
the Duke is a story that might inspire such a
grim and terrible poetic tragedy as *The Duchess
of Malfi*. For the Duchess of Praslin's only
crime, in her husband's eyes, seems to have
been that of loving him too well, and of making
him aware, partly by reproachful speech and
partly by her written word, how keenly she
felt the change which came after seventeen
years of exceptionally happy married life.

There was, as we shall see, another woman in
the case ; and not the least strange and interesting part of the story is that of the connection
of the Duke and of this woman, whom no
reasonable being suspected even in France,
where such things are easily suspected, of

having done the Duchess any real wrong as a wife.

The curious and pitiful story aroused deep interest and discussion all over Europe, and the English memoirs and collections of letters written at the time contain many allusions to the affair.

At half-past four on one August morning in 1847, a couple of workmen, passing down the deserted Rue Saint-Honoré, heard piercing screams proceeding from behind the high walls of Marshal Sabatiani's splendid town house. The Marshal was a popular Parisian—a survival of the glorious Napoleonic régime—and his only child, as all the world knew, was the Duchess of Praslin.

Though it was August, the great mansion was now peopled, for the Duke and Duchess and their numerous children had arrived the evening before to spend a couple of nights in Paris, on their way to the seaside.

Those horrible, unnatural cries of agony and terror proceeded from the Duchess's bedroom, and two of the servants—the Duchess's maid and the Duke's valet—roused by the sounds, had risen in haste and rushed to the various doors giving access to the suite of apartments occupied by their mistress. These doors they found were all locked.

Now, the Duchess's bedroom, the principal

bed-chamber of the house, was a magnificent apartment, copied from Marie Antoinette's bed-chamber at Versailles. Of its four doors, one gave into the Duchess's boudoir ; the second on to a public staircase ; the third into a dressing-room ; and the fourth led into a small ante-chamber which separated her bed-chamber from that of the Duke. This private ante-chamber could also be reached by a small staircase from below, and it was up this staircase that the two servants finally raced breathlessly, to find that, alone of the four doors giving on the Duchess's bed-chamber, this door was unlocked.

" Madame la Duchesse ! What is the matter ? " they cried.

But there came no answering moan or sign. Cautiously feeling their way as they went, for the room was in complete darkness, they walked forward into the vast bedroom, and as they advanced there struck on their nostrils a horrible smell—the smell of freshly spilt blood.

With awkward, trembling fingers, the faithful maid—who had been with her mistress since the day when the Duchess had left this very house as a radiant bride of sixteen—drew back the thick silk curtains which draped the windows, and as she did so an awful sight met her eyes and those of the valet.

Amid a scene of horrible confusion, heavy furniture upset, bed-curtains torn down, and

splashes of blood everywhere, the Duchess of
Praslin lay on the floor, crouching against a low
chair, and wearing only a blood-stained night-
gown. If not then dead, she was on the point
of death, for she remained motionless, and no
sound came from her lips.

Neither the man nor the woman dared
approach the prostrate figure ; instead, they
backed out of the room (noticing as they went
that all was still in the Duke's bed-chamber),
and roused their fellow-servants.

Soon the whole household was gathered in
the great drawing-room, debating in quick
whispers who should undertake the painful
task of waking the Duke.

The problem was solved by their master
himself. Suddenly he stood among them—a
haggard, horror-stricken figure still clad in his
night-dress. For a few moments those who
crowded respectfully round him supposed him
ignorant of the tragedy, for, "What is the
matter?" he cried. "What has happened to
bring you all here?"

Telling him of the awful discovery which had
been made, the valet adventured the theory that
the house had been broken into by burglars,
and the Duchess murdered with a view to
securing her jewels, which were very fine, and
which included a wonderful set of diamonds
given to her mother by Napoleon and Josephine.

The Duke of Praslin at once ordered the police and a doctor to be summoned, and sent about their various business the distracted household. Then, and not till then, he made his way to his wife's room.

There he was heard to exclaim, " Good God, how horrible! My poor Fanny! What monster has done this thing ? "

In an agony of grief, he threw himself on the wide empty bed, crying out: " Alas! alas! my motherless children! Who is to tell them of the awful thing that has happened ? "

But he did not touch his wife's dead body, and finally, leaving her where she lay, he retired to his own room.

A few moments later the police arrived, and then every member of the large household had to submit to a severe examination ; for when such a tragedy takes place it is the inmates of the house who are first suspected, if not of having actually committed the crime, of being at least accomplices and accessories.

What greatly added to the horror of this particular murder was the dreadful brutality with which the Duchess had been done to death.

The fine carved and gilt bed—which stood, as is the custom in French state bed-chambers, on a platform above the floor—was in fearful confusion, the pillows deeply stained with blood, as were also the curtains.

It was clear that there had been a terrible struggle between the Duchess and her murderer or murderers. Not only had she received five gaping wounds, any one of which would have been fatal, but her face and neck were covered with deep scratches.

On being first attacked, the Duchess had evidently leaped out of bed to face her assailants, and, though already severely wounded, she had tried in the darkness to find the door to her boudoir,—for round three sides of the great room ran bloody finger-marks.

Finally she had been dragged violently into the middle of the room, for on various pieces of furniture were found strands of her long, beautiful hair.

The only clue that the police found—but they attached great importance to it—was a pistol, to the handle of which adhered several of the Duchess's hairs and a small piece of skin.

At first it was supposed that the murderers had gained their entrance into the house by the garden giving on the Champs Élysées; but all the gates on that side were found to be securely fastened from within.

After every member of the household had been questioned and cross-questioned with the pitiless intellectual ferocity usual to the French detective force, the Duke of Praslin was asked to tell what he knew of the events of the previous night.

And then came the first great surprise of the case.

The Duke at once calmly revealed the fact that he had known of the murder before the servants had told him of it. Waked by his wife's screams, he had rushed into the Duchess's room, to find her dead. Stunned by the sight, he had gone back to his own room. He also casually mentioned that the pistol which had been regarded as so important a clue to the murder was *his* pistol, brought into the room when he first heard the cries of his wife, and there forgotten by him in his horror and confusion.

This strange statement seems to have been at first received with respectful belief; and the next step taken by the police was thoroughly to search the servants' rooms. While this was being done, one of them was heard to mutter: " It would be more to the purpose to search the Duke's room."

This hint was acted upon, and the Duke's bedchamber was found to be in a very curious state. The fireplace was choked with papers which a recent attempt had evidently been made to burn. A silk jacket which the Duke wore at night, and which he had evidently tried to destroy, was also found in the fireplace. In the dressing-closet, thrust into a dark cupboard, was a dressing-gown completely soaked in blood.

As a result of these discoveries, the magistrate who had charge of the investigation was brought at last to realize that the only human being in the house against whom there existed any presumption of guilt was the husband of the victim !

II

Now, the Duke of Praslin was not only a great peer, descended from the oldest French nobility and allied, through his wife, to the powerful new Napoleonic caste, but he was also a man of high personal character. Heir to a great name and immense wealth, he had chosen, when only one-and-twenty, to make a *mariage d'amour*. His family, it was well known, had not approved of his choice; for, though Mademoiselle Sabatiani was beautiful, accomplished, and also very wealthy, she belonged to that new nobility which was then, as now, despised by the old.

It was further known to the police—each Frenchman above a certain social status has every particular concerning his or her past registered in a *dossier*—that the Duke had shown himself not only a devoted, but a most faithful husband.

It seemed inconceivable that such a man should have murdered the woman he had married for love, and who, still young, still beautiful—she was thirty-five at the time of her death—was the mother of his nine children.

And so we cannot wonder that the long day which had begun at four in the morning passed very painfully, for suspicions accumulated with each hour against the Duke. There were found in his dressing-room a hunting-knife, a poniard, and a short sword stained with blood.

At last, to his deep revolt and anger, the Duke of Praslin was made to submit to a close physical examination. It was then found that his hands were covered with scratches, and that one of his arms had been bitten.

All these proofs—for by now they were accounted to be proofs—were laid before the King. But Louis Philippe hesitated to sign the warrant of arrest. It was a serious thing at this particular moment of French history, on the eve of the revolution of 1848, to order the arrest of a great peer on so terrible a charge as that of murdering his wife.

Meanwhile an examination was made of the half-burnt papers found in the Duke's fireplace, and these at last provided what had until then been completely lacking, namely, a motive for the crime. These papers proved to be letters, and, together with others that were soon found both in the Duke's rooms and in the Duchess's locked desk, they made it clear that the unhappy woman had loved her husband so jealously as to torture them both.

Why, my beloved, have you changed to me? Why have you become, not only cold, but indifferent? Why have you taken away from our joint life all the happiness and all the brightness of mutual love? You say you wish to be independent—but do you also wish to live alone? You say that I am unreasonable because I wish to share your sorrows and your anxieties. But it is you who are unreasonable in wishing to make of me a stranger. How long is it since you turned against the woman you once loved with so mad and absorbing a passion? I am filled with anguish—my heart is broken. You say you are grieved at seeing me look sad, but it is you—you, Theo—who have made me sad. You know—no one better—how easy it would be to make me glad! But you refused to do the very little that I ask. Am I not your comrade, the sharer of your life, the half of yourself,—she who has the right as well as the duty of consoling you when you are sad, and of laughing with you when you are glad? You were ill not long ago, and yet you refused to allow me to nurse you! Is it because I am

violent that you avoid me ? And yet, when
I was a younger woman, you never minded
my violence—my occasional bursts of bad
temper.

And then, in another letter:

The last four months have taught me
that I was wrong, unreasonable to try and
force your confidence. I recognize how
infinitely superior is your character and
nature to mine ; I only ask most humbly to
go on sharing your life. I declare on all
that I hold most sacred and most dear—my
children—that I will henceforth only ask
you for your love, your kindness. Forgive
your Fanny any impatience or annoyance
she may have caused you, Theo ! I have
heard it whispered that you were seeking
distractions outside your home. Ah, my
dear, no one will make you as happy as I
made you happy in the old, old days ! A
man of your character, with your heart and
your ideals, will never be content with low
and venal loves. Your wife has no other
happiness, no other ideal, no other thought
in the world but you. Oh, do not shut
your ears to her prayers, to her humble
devotion. She loves you, Theo ; and if
only you will forgive her anything she may
have done to offend you, she will never so
offend you again.
    See her waiting day and night at your
door, afraid to come in ; afraid even to

knock! Think of our blissful past; think of our children, whom we both love so dearly. And yet, Theodore, I have a right to be hurt, even to be jealous of my children, for you seem now to love them more than you do their mother. You are certainly more with them than you are with her. But then, you never are with her——

To a secret diary, which was found in their country home, the unhappy woman confided even more plainly her sorrow, anger, and jealousy.

For a considerable time this jealousy was not attached to any one object or objects; it was only the outcome of a passionate sense of loss, blended with inconsistent bursts of devotion and tenderness.

Two years have gone by. All my hopes are now shattered. I feel that he has become quite indifferent to me. He simply no longer loves me. Sometimes he seems to feel a positive aversion for the woman he once loved so passionately. And then again I realize that he does not think of me at all—or, rather, he thinks of me only when I force him to do so by my cries and my complaints.

For many years I was first in his heart, first in his thoughts—ever in his thoughts. And then suddenly everything changed. And now it has grown worse. Until a few weeks ago, whenever he entered the house, however late, he always came in to see me for a few minutes. Now he goes straight to his own apartments. And yet he promised me so faithfully at least to keep up these usual, kindly ways of commonplace married life.

I have kept a letter from him in which he says: "If you will not come to me, for I dislike very much to be disturbed, I promise you I will come to you." I kept my promise, for never once have I gone and sought him out when he was busy or tired; but he has quite given up coming in to me as he used to do. He does not even ask me for a cup of tea. We do not even breakfast or lunch together.

And then again in the same hidden diary:

He goes out on foot, not driving or riding, as he used to do. If only I knew the truth I should feel more calm. But alas! I shall never know the truth; he is so reserved, so silent, so secretive.

There follows a most pathetic entry:

Theo has changed again! The other day he was really tender in his manner. He implied that he wished to change our strange way of life. But is this really true? Does he wish to restore me to my natural position as his wife, and as the mother of my children? Does he realize that if this comes to pass I shall not be content with less than everything? *He will have to dismiss Mademoiselle D.*

Here we have mentioned for the first time the woman who was to play so disastrous a part in the last years of the Duchess's life, and whose existence undoubtedly contributed in a great measure to her death; that is, always supposing that the Duke of Praslin did kill his wife.

III

The person to whom the Duchess of Praslin in her diary referred as "Mademoiselle D." was Henriette Deluzy, governess to the children of the Duke and Duchess.

At the time that Mademoiselle Deluzy had the misfortune to obtain what seemed so excellent a post, she was a quiet, thoughtful, intelligent woman of thirty. She had been for five years in England as the trusted governess of a Lady Hislop; and when she went to France that lady gave her the highest character that one woman could give to another.

Henriette Deluzy had a gentle, composed manner; she was a good musician; she knew several languages; and, above all, she was quite willing to lead the dull life that is the lot of most governesses.

It was the Duke, not the Duchess, who engaged her. He explained that his wife was not in good health, and that he was thus obliged to concern himself with the education of their children. He offered Mademoiselle Deluzy two thousand francs (£80) a year, with the proviso that if she stayed with the family till the elder daughters were married she would receive a pension of fifteen hundred francs (£60) during the rest of her life.

The Duke made certain strict stipulations. The governess had to bind herself never to leave the children alone, and she was to have no holidays. No wonder the lady whose place she was taking drew for her a rather melancholy picture of the life she was about to lead. Her predecessor also confided to Mademoiselle Deluzy that the Duke and Duchess were on very bad terms with each other, though outwardly united. But the new governess, being a sensible woman, did not attach much importance to the information, since she did not suppose that she would have much to do, in a personal way, with the parents of her pupils.

But it is impossible to live in a household with two other human beings and not play some part in their lives. Very soon the governess discovered that she must needs take sides. She took the side of the Duke, for he saw a great deal of his children, and showed the deepest interest in their lessons, their games, and in the training of their young minds.

The Duchess, it must be admitted, did none of these things. She passionately loved her children, but she was absorbed—as the letters and the diary we have quoted show—in herself, in her grief, in her jealousy and pain. And so, from the point of view of Mademoiselle Deluzy, the father was far more admirable as a parent than was the mother of her pupils.

Another thing. The Duke gradually found pleasure in the governess's intelligent conversation. Mademoiselle Deluzy cared for public affairs, for literature, for a hundred and one things to which the ordinary pretty woman gives little thought. And, as time went on, the father of her pupils spent more and more of his leisure in the schoolroom, and, when in the country, in walking with his children and their governess.

Thus was created another complication in the unfortunate Duchess's relations with her husband. She became agonizingly jealous of the governess, though even she recognized that the Duke was not in love with Mademoiselle Deluzy. From being angered by the fact that the Duke had formed the habit of going out alone without saying where he was going, the Duchess now was furious because he stayed so much at home.

Very soon we find her writing this in her secret diary :

> Were I to ask Theo to choose between myself and Mademoiselle Deluzy, I cannot help thinking that he would choose her.

And again :

> All is finished.   We have quarrelled ! How strange that he should now have such an aversion for the wife who loves him so purely, so tenderly, so devotedly !   Doubtless my character is not a very easy one. But whose fault is it that I get into such states that I sometimes act as if I were mad ?

And then this outburst of anguish :

> When I walk to the front door through which you took me on our wedding-day, a day when I was so full of joy and love and hope—when I go into those rooms in which we dwelt together when you loved me, when you never liked to leave me even for an hour, a terrible feeling of agony, of chill despair, comes over me. . . . Instead of fearing, as so many women do, old age, I used to look forward to the evening of our days.   I used to think we would talk over our youth—that we would live once more in our children, and that in the end we would die and go to a better land together.

In yet another letter to her husband, the
wretched woman gives an account of what must
have been a degrading scene :

> Yes, it is quite true ! I did behave in a
> very undignified and foolish way this after-
> noon. When I came in and found you
> sitting there, talking with Mademoiselle D.,
> discussing your political future with a
> woman who is less than nothing to either
> of us, I confess I lost my head, and I admit
> that I behaved in a way that was unwomanly
> and silly. I rushed out of the room.
> . . . But what did you do ? You followed
> me in such a state of fury that, for the first
> time in my life, Theo, I felt afraid —afraid
> of you, my only love. You came into my
> boudoir, and what did you do there ? You
> broke a valuable object, a beautiful vase
> that you had given me when we were still
> happy together. Ah, yes, you did punish
> me, truly !
>
> The other day, when I went to see the
> Queen, her lady-in-waiting, that kindly
> Madame Dololieu, said to me : " Your hus-
> band is very tenderly devoted to you, is
> he not ? " And I had to say. " Yes." I had
> to smile.

IV

We learn little of the character and nature of
the Duke of Praslin. The Duchess lives again
in her portraits—hers is a rather imperious beauty

—in her letters, and in her diary ; but the Duke remains an enigma. He does not seem ever to have answered any of his wife's outpourings or pleadings for sympathy. Had he done so, she would certainly have kept his letters. Only one scrap of paper in the Duke's handwriting was found after the tragedy, and, as we shall see, it contained but one terrible sentence.

It is clear that the Duke opposed, to all his wife's passionate appeals, what is perhaps the only weapon a husband so situated can use— the weapon of silent obstinacy. In the letter last quoted we see his kind of dumb patience tried too high ; we see him showing the rage that possessed him ; and it is significant that on that one occasion he lost all command of himself, and made his wife, as she wrote in her pathetic letter, for the first time in her life, afraid.

On all ordinary occasions it is plain that the Duke so treated the Duchess in public as to give the impression to those about them that he was still fondly attached to her.

She, on her side, also kept her own counsel, and she seems to have had only two confidants —a man and a woman of her own world. She received from them the sensible advice it is so easy to give in such a case, and so very, very difficult to follow. They told her what is always so plain to the on-looker, that no wife, no lover, can ever win back or revive cooling affection by making scenes, by writing piteous letters, by showing herself jealous.

But this advice, so kindly meant, and more than once conveyed in really fine and eloquent language—for those were the days when people were fond of writing long letters to one another —had no effect.

The Duke can hardly ever have come home, hardly ever have gone into his study, or even into his bed-chamber, without receiving from the Duchess some harrowing missive, reproachful, threatening, or cajoling by turns :

> You told me the day before yesterday something which pierced my heart. You said that, as I had nothing to do with any of your public concerns, I had no right to share your intimate sorrows. Yes ; you wish us to be real strangers the one to the other. If that be so, then let me say farewell. Be happy, if you can be happy ! You have our children — I have nothing ! Your hatred, perhaps I should say your indifference, has taken all from me. And I would rather be hated than suffer your indifference.

Again :

> I am dying of grief ! For five long years, I have spent all my nights in tears, in convulsions of sorrow. Often I have

had to bite my pillow in order to stifle my
sobs, my cries.

I have lost not only my husband but
my children. I suffer the tortures of
Tantalus. I am close to you all, and yet
I am apart from you all !

Why, it may reasonably be asked by those
who think that a man-made law can alter human
nature, did not these two unhappy people part
company? They remained together, united in
appearance, for the very sufficient reason that the
Duchess had no wish to leave the man she so
passionately loved. More than once she suggested going away, and she threatened to make
a public scandal. But, when it came to the
point, she found she could not bring herself to
do it. Ever we find in her letters the pleadings
of a woman who cannot believe that she is
no longer loved. Constantly we hear the cry,
springing from the depths of her suffering heart,
expressed in such words as these :

Something surely will happen to make
you love me again, as you loved me once ?
It is impossible that you have changed as
much as you seem to have changed !

And then, as time went on, the Duchess became
more actively jealous of Mademoiselle Deluzy,
and more determined that the governess should

leave the house.   She discovered, or thought
she   discovered, that the servants thought it
very strange that the Duke spent so much of
his spare time in the schoolroom.

At last she took the grave step of asking
her father, Marshal Sabatiani, to interfere in the
matter. The old man, after hearing his daughter's
account of what was going on, wrote a very
dignified letter to the Duke:

> The day will come when you will be
> sorry for having behaved as you are now
> doing. Surely it is your duty to consider
> your wife's feelings in so important a
> matter—to say nothing of the duty you
> owe to your daughters; for, however in-
> nocent you may be, there is no doubt that
> your relations to this woman are being very
> much discussed in your household.
>
> I am perfectly willing to do whatever
> is fair and right by this lady—indeed, I
> will myself settle so large a pension on
> her that she will no longer have to work
> for her living.

Very reluctantly, with a heavy heart, and
one also full of the bitterest revolt and anger
against his wife, the Duke of Praslin had to
give way, and it was arranged that Mademoiselle
Deluzy should leave at the end of the summer
term.

But the Duchess had won a sterile victory.

The Duke sent her a note containing only this
curt line:

" By your act you have spoilt my life."

And in her diary of the 17th of June, before
leaving her country home for the fatal stay in
Paris, the Duchess wrote :

> The only thing I can tell myself is that
> I did my duty, not only to myself, but also
> to my daughters. For a long time I
> hesitated. God knows I hesitated a long
> time before I allowed my father to act.
> Oh, God, I fear the future! How angry
> Theo is! One would say that it is I, not
> he, who is guilty. Oh, God, I beg you to
> open my husband's eyes. He is already
> weary of this woman. He is afraid of her.
> It is his pride which makes him full of anger
> and rage. As for me, he will never forgive
> me. I fear that some day he will revenge
> himself on me. The pit which has been
> digged between us is becoming deeper and
> deeper. The future frightens me. I tremble
> when I think of it.

And just fifteen days before her foul murder
she wrote :

> Nothing has changed. *She* has not yet
> gone. She has the father and the children
> entirely in her power. They are plunged
> in grief at her approaching departure, and I
> am made to feel a criminal.

4

V

Mademoiselle Deluzy left the Duke of Praslin's country house within a very few days after these lines were written, and then there happened a most extraordinary thing, of which no mention will be found in any of the published accounts of the tragic drama, but which is still whispered in French society.

Two nights before the family were to move to Paris, the Duchess, who always slept badly, was heard by her maid just after dawn to give a loud and terrible scream.

Without even waiting to put on a gown, the woman rushed to her mistress's room. To her surprise, she found the door locked on the inside. After a few moments, she tried the door again, and this time found it unlocked.

The Duchess was sitting up in bed, a look of awful fear on her face.

" What is it, Madame la Duchesse ? "

" I had an awful nightmare "—and the Duchess shivered. " Waking up suddenly, I seemed to see advancing toward me—the Devil ! He was dressed, as the Devil always is dressed, in bright red from head to foot. He crept nearer and nearer, and I gave a loud scream. Then I heard a click—and he vanished into the wall ! "

At the time that this happened, the maid did not tell anybody of the strange episode ; she thought that her mistress had had an evil dream, and that in the course of her dream she had first locked the door and then unlocked it.

But a year later, when the doubly orphaned children of the Duke and Duchess of Praslin came back to their country home, there was found in a little cupboard which filled up the short passage between the Duke and Duchess's former apartments, a fancy dress worn by the Duke in early youth.

The dress was that of Mephistopheles—bright red from head to foot; and in its folds was wrapped a sharp, pointed dagger.

VI

Owing to the Duke of Praslin's high rank, and to the fact that there was only presumptive evidence of guilt—for he continued, it need hardly be said, to deny with cold dignity the awful accusation brought against him—he was not watched with the care he should have been, before being transferred from his own house to prison. And within an hour of his arrest he managed to swallow a large dose of poison.

For a while nothing was suspected. The Duke grew very ill; but the police supposed this to be due to his agitation of mind, and so did his family doctor.

Meanwhile—for in the France of that day, as

in the England of this, a peer of the realm could only be judged by his peers—the French House of Peers was hurriedly summoned.

Six men of his own rank, many of whom he had known since childhood, came and placed themselves round the bed on which the Duke now lay in agony; and the Lord Chancellor of the kingdom, Pasquier, began the interrogation:

"You know the awful crime of which you are accused? You know the circumstances which have led to your being suspected? I beg—I implore you, Duke, to tell us the truth."

The Duke answered:

"I have not the strength to say anything. It would take a long time for me to tell you the truth, and nothing but the truth."

"You say that it would take a long time to tell the truth. We do not ask you to tell us the whole truth; we want only a 'yes' or a 'no.'"

The Duke replied:

"It requires great strength of mind to be able to say 'yes' or 'no' to certain questions, and it is a strength which I do not now possess."

"Well, tell us one thing,—at what hour did you leave your children on the night before the crime was committed?"

"It must have been half-past ten—perhaps a little earlier."

" What did you then do ? "

" I went into my bedroom and at once proceeded to get into bed."

" Did you sleep ? "

The Duke sighed deeply and replied, " Yes."

" Had you made up your mind when you went to bed what you would do in the morning ? "

" I do not know what you mean by asking me this question."

" When you awoke, what was your first thought ? "

" I heard cries in the house, and I rushed into my wife's room."

The Duke moaned, and added : " Cannot you wait awhile before continuing your questions ? I feel so very weak."

" No; we cannot accede to your wish. By telling us the truth you will shorten the interrogation. When you went into the Duchess's room, you must at once have seen what had happened. Did you find her in bed ? "

" No. I have already said that she was lying on the ground."

" Whence came the scratches and the bites with which your hands are covered ? "

" They happened the night before. But I beg you to spare me these questions. I am getting weaker and weaker."

" You must feel very distressed at having committed so awful a crime ? "

The accused man made no answer, and indeed he did seem too ill to answer.

Then came a question which involved another human being:

" Did you not receive some bad advice which urged you to commit this crime ? "

And, to everyone's amazement, the Duke of Praslin roused himself and replied in a strong voice:

" Nay, indeed! I received no counsel from anyone. Who would have counselled such a thing ? "

" Are you not devoured by remorse ? Would it not be a certain relief to tell us the truth ? "

" I am without any strength to-day."

" You speak constantly of your lack of strength; but we ask you only to say ' yes ' or ' no.' "

" If someone would feel my pulse, he would see how very ill I am."

" And yet you were strong enough just now to declare most firmly that no one had advised you to commit this frightful crime."

The Duke remained silent.

" We seek only the truth."

" On the contrary, you came here feeling already quite sure that I was guilty. It is impossible for me now to change your view."

And, indeed, the unhappy man was so ill that the questioning had to be abandoned.

All through that night he suffered tortures of pain, but he made no complaint.

In the morning, after the accused had seen his confessor, the Duke of Decazes, who had been the dying man's great friend, was begged to approach him once more.

" I fear you suffer greatly, my poor Praslin," said Decazes.

" Yes."

" But it is your own fault, is it not, that you are suffering ? You took poison."

The Duke of Praslin did not answer.

" Is it laudanum you took ? "

" No."

" Then you took arsenic ? "

" Yes," said the dying man, lifting his head.

" Who got you this arsenic ? "

" No one got it. I brought it from Praslin."

There was a moment's silence.

Then the Duke of Decazes made a last appeal to his friend and comrade.

" Now is the time, now is the moment—for your own sake, for that of your name, of your family, as regards your memory, your children— to speak. The fact that you poisoned yourself is tantamount to a confession. A man who is innocent does not choose the moment when his nine children have been deprived of their mother to deprive them also of their father. Admit that you are guilty ! "

The Duke of Praslin remained silent.

" At any rate, do you regret your crime ?   Tell me that you regret what you have done ! "

The Duke, with an expression of terrible anguish, repeated the words : " Do I regret ? "

" I beg of you to tell the truth.   Receive the Chancellor and confess what happened ! "

The dying man hesitated.   " No," he said slowly.   " I am too feeble, but perhaps I will see the Chancellor to-morrow."

Decazes had not the heart to insist.   And then he took down, at the other's dictation, a curious little statement, in no sense a confession :

" I wish to say how much I regret I cannot see my children before I die.   I implore my family to be kind to them all.   I have not had time to make any arrangements with regard to my fortune.   I am happy to leave my children in the care of my beloved old mother.   I beg them not to follow too closely the counsels of their uncles and of their grandfather Sabatiani. I left at home a will, which I now ratify.   It was made some time ago.   I am happy to think that my mother will be there to take care of my daughters.   I wish my sons to remain at the schools where they are now."

" I ask you once more," said the Duke of Decazes, " if you are guilty of the crime of killing your wife ? "

" No, Monsieur le Duc, I do not admit that I am guilty."

" But, if you are not guilty, why did you poison yourself? "

" I am not guilty."

And then at last there was uttered by the questioner the name of the woman who unwittingly had played so great a part in the tragedy, and who had been arrested and put in prison " au secret."

" Did Mademoiselle Deluzy give you any advice which made you commit the awful deed which we feel sure you have committed ? "

And the Duke, dying though he was, raised himself to his elbow : " No, no ! Mademoiselle Deluzy never dreamt of such a thing ! "

" Once more I ask you, did you commit this crime ? "

" No, Decazes. I will never tell you that I am guilty."

Half an hour later the Duke of Praslin expired in agony, or so at least it was publicly given out. But it is still believed by many Parisians that the Duke recovered, and that he was allowed to leave the country in disguise.

It is said that he lived in England, to extreme old age, in the enjoyment of a handsome income which was regularly transmitted to him first by his eldest son, and later by his grandson.

4*

VII

And now the only real point of interrogation that remains is Mademoiselle Deluzy. Under that quiet, correct exterior, what manner of woman was the governess?

For a while—indeed, for a considerable time—the French police were inclined to believe that she had been the Duke's accomplice. They even went so far as to think it possible that she had been in the house on that fatal night, and that she had actually helped to do the unhappy Duchess to death. As for the public, so exasperated were they that the market-women of Paris threatened to lynch her.

But, in spite of the deep prejudice against her, Mademoiselle Deluzy, by her calmness, her good sense, and her dignity, soon altered the point of view of those whose duty it was to investigate her part in the tragic story.

She answered every question put to her frankly and simply; and though it was clear that she had had a not unreasonable prejudice against the Duchess, she tried to be as fair as was possible, and in one of her answers we have what is probably the truest pen portrait of that unhappy woman.

" I do not wish to be lacking in respect to the memory of the Duchess of Praslin; but, if you ask me for the truth, I will tell the truth. I do not accuse her heart; I do not accuse her sentiments—but she had a most difficult and un-happy nature. She was incapable of managing her children. When with them, she by turns irritated and spoiled them. She was weak when she ought to have been severe ; unkind when she ought to have been indulgent ; cruel when she ought to have been kind. *She was far too preoccupied with the feelings that animated her for her husband* to give much thought to anything else in the world!"

Henriette Deluzy was kept in prison for three months, and in those twelve weeks of anguish and fear she changed, as regarded her personal appearance, from that of a young to that of a middle-aged woman. At last it was decided that as there was really no evidence against her she must be set at liberty. This was accordingly done, and a day or two later it was rumoured that Mademoiselle Deluzy had gone to England. This, however, was not true. She stayed in France, under an assumed name, for some time, and then, on the advice of the highly-respected Protestant pastor, M. Monod, who had been her valued friend for many years, she went to America, to take a place as teacher in Miss Page's celebrated school in Grammercy Park.

Time went on, and at the house of Miss Page Mademoiselle Deluzy made the acquaintance of a certain Mr. Henry Field, well known in New York literary and legal circles. He fell in love with her, and made her an offer of marriage.

And there came the painful moment when she had to tell him of her strange and dreadful connection with the Praslin affair.

The story made no difference to the American's generous heart. Mademoiselle Deluzy, however, considered him entitled to an impartial statement of what had taken place, and she wrote to the noted literary man, Victor Cousin, in order to obtain such a statement.

Giving him her lover's address, she begged him to write and tell him the truth. " You know the whole story," she wrote. " You were even present once when I was being questioned by the police. You have read all the Duchess's letters, and those of my letters that were found. I do not ask for pity—I ask you simply to tell the truth as a man of honour."

M. Cousin wrote to Mr. Field, and very soon afterwards the marriage took place.

Mr. and Mrs. Henry Field took up their residence in Massachusetts, and the French-woman became an intimate friend of Mrs. Harriet Beecher Stowe. She died in 1874, and after her death a book by her was published, entitled " Familiar Sketches of France," but she left no record of the strange and dreadful story with which she had been so closely associated, and not even to her closest friends had the name of Praslin ever passed her lips.

III

NOT PROVEN: MADELEINE SMITH

NOT PROVEN: MADELEINE SMITH

I

On a cold, fine day late in March, 1857, in the handsome drawing-room of No. 7, Blythswood Square, Glasgow, sat a still young-looking mother and her elder daughter. They were Mrs. James Smith, the wife of a prosperous architect, and Madeleine Smith, a girl of twenty, distinguished, even beyond the confines of the city in which she dwelt, for her exceptional loveliness, her vivacity, and her charm of manner.

The many sketches which were later to be made of this Scottish girl give no notion of what she was really like, but one who knew her during her unshadowed youth has described her as of medium height and extremely graceful; he noted, as perhaps her most attractive features, her eyes, which were large and true blue in colour, and shaded by long lashes. It is also on record that on that fateful March day her whole being seemed instinct with health and the zest of life.

The mother's gaze rested tenderly on her eldest

child, for the date of Madeleine's forthcoming wedding had been fixed only the day before.

Her parents were well pleased at the marriage ; their prospective son-in-law, William Minnoch, was not only prosperous in business, but he was also a man of high character, one to whom they could with confidence entrust their cherished eldest daughter.

The whole household were in a joyful, busy state, and that perhaps was why Mr. James Smith came in and out of the drawing-room so often that day, addressing kindly words to his wife, and gazing affectionately on the young daughter who was so soon to leave him.

As her parents' glances rested on Madeleine, they called to mind how well she had behaved some two years before, when, to please them, she had given up an unsuitable love affair with a young foreigner named Angelier. Madeleine had shown herself a good, dutiful daughter on that occasion, for she had certainly been more or less in love—in so far as a child of seventeen can be in love—with Émile Angelier. Her father had kept a copy of the letter which Madeleine had written to a certain Miss Perry, who had acted as go-between and confidante in that unsuitable love affair :

My papa will not give his consent, and I am in duty bound to obey him. Comfort

dear Émile! I had hoped some day to
have been happy with him, but, alas! we
were doomed to be disappointed. I hope and
trust he may prosper. I am glad he is
leaving the country, for it would have caused
me great pain to have met him. Think my
conduct not unkind. I have a father to
study, and a kind father, too.

Yes, in the eyes of her fond parents Madeleine had behaved very well over that matter—
indeed, in a way that might serve as an example
to many a rebellious daughter.

Suddenly there came the sound of the front-
door bell.

" A visitor, my dear," said Mr. Smith, and,
man-like, hastily left the room.

A moment later Miss Perry was shown up,
the very woman who had played what most sensible people would agree to have been a foolish
and even a reprehensible part in Madeleine's
former love-affair.

Mother and daughter glanced at each other.
They could well have dispensed with a visitor
this afternoon, and particularly with this visitor.
Madeleine had been but slightly acquainted with
Miss Perry, and her only association with her
was not pleasant. Still, Mrs. Smith and her
daughter greeted the unwelcome visitor civilly.

After a few moments of aimless talk Miss
Perry exclaimed:

"I had a serious reason for coming here this afternoon, Mrs. Smith, or I would not have troubled you with a call. I feel that you ought to know that Émile Angelier is dead. He died last night, very suddenly, having sent me a message to say he was ill and desired to see me. But when I reached his lodgings he had already passed away."

There was a moment's painful pause. Then Mrs. Smith expressed her regret at the news. Madeleine flushed deeply, but did not seem very seriously affected. And Miss Perry, in some confusion, rose and stiffly took her leave.

The scene was characteristic. All three ladies in the unpleasant circumstances showed a true Scottish reticence, and no word was spoken of past events.

But let us look into their hearts. Mrs. Smith, though rather shocked at her own feeling, must have felt a certain measure of relief that Angelier was dead. The episode of his love-affair had caused the only cloud that had ever passed between herself and her elder daughter.

And Madeleine? What were her feelings on learning the news of her one-time "dear Émile's" death. Whatever secret was hidden behind those lovely, downcast blue eyes, we may suppose that she now only remembered that Angelier had truly loved her.

As for Miss Perry—well, she, it is clear, was

seized with far more violent feelings of pain and distress, and her stiff behaviour showed as clearly as the plainest speech would have done how indignant she was at the coldness of both mother and daughter.

It is on record that Miss Perry lingered for a moment in the entrance hall of Mr. James Smith's comfortable house, wondering whether Madeleine would run down after her to learn something more of the pitiful end of her erstwhile lover. And as she thus lingered, Miss Perry also seems to have asked herself whether she ought to tell the girl that certain letters had been found among the dead man's belongings.

But Madeleine Smith remained upstairs with her mother, and so at last the door of No. 7, Blythswood Square closed behind the unbidden guest.

The rest of that afternoon whiled itself away in busy nothings. The family—consisting of five sons and daughters—met at the evening meal, attended family prayers, and later bade one another good night and went to bed, Madeleine, and the little sister who slept with her, retiring to the curious half-basement room which, by the elder girl's own wish, had always been hers since the Smiths had moved into their new house.

Next morning, at five o'clock, while it was

still quite dark, Madeleine got up, hurriedly
dressed herself, and slipped out of the house,
taking with her only a small carpet bag. Through
the empty, lamplit streets she crept quietly to
catch the early boat that was the first stage of
the journey to her father's country house at
Rowalyn.

But the unhappy girl—for henceforth we may
truly call her unhappy—was not allowed to go
far. By the time the sun had well risen, all
Glasgow was ringing with the news that Madeleine Smith, the beautiful young daughter of
one of the most respected citizens of the town,
and the betrothed of another, had been arrested
on the awful charge of "having on two separate
occasions administered arsenic, or some other
poison, to Émile Angelier, with intent to murder
him, and of having actually murdered him on
the second occasion."

II

The long train of extraordinary events which
culminated in the death of the unfortunate
Angelier sprang from a very trifling incident.

Strolling one day along Sauchiehall Street, the
Oxford Street of Glasgow, a young Frenchman,
employed in the humble capacity of correspondence clerk in a Glasgow business house, saw a
very pretty girl pass by.

He spoke to her, only to be spurned with proper dignity. Completely bewitched, however, he followed her and discovered where she lived. Then, on learning that she was the daughter of a citizen of repute and substance, he left no stone unturned to obtain an introduction to her, and finally effected his purpose through the good offices of the French Consul-General.

Émile Angelier soon became very much in love, but he realized that Mr. James Smith would never consent to receive him as a suitor for Madeleine. He persuaded the girl, nevertheless, to meet him clandestinely at the house of his friend Miss Perry. A few love-letters were exchanged, and one of these fell into the hands of Mrs. Smith. Madeleine's parents—not unreasonably, when we consider her youth and the difference of position between their daughter and Angelier—put an end, not sternly, but kindly and firmly, to the affair.

But Angelier was not minded to let go his beautiful prey so easily. Not only was he now passionately in love, but a marriage with Madeleine Smith would lift him out of his lowly condition. He knew himself to be well educated, refined, and intelligent. Why should he not have the good fortune of the many men who have found in a rich marriage the necessary lift up fortune's ladder?

Angelier had already worked his way from

a poor and destitute position to one that was respectable, and a credit to himself. He knew he was liked by his employers, and he believed himself to be popular among his fellow-clerks.

Once more he persuaded Madeleine to renew, in solemn fashion, their clandestine engagement. Again they met at the house of Miss Perry, who seems to have delighted in the rôle of go-between. They spent blissful hours in the greater privacy, the free solitude, of the woods which abounded round the Smiths' country home at Rowalyn. And, finally, after their acquaintance had lasted rather more than a year, Madeleine Smith, by word and by deed, had completely committed herself to the young Frenchman.

For a while, great as was the evil he wrought, Angelier behaved as a man of honour, according to the Continental code of honour, should behave to the woman who has given herself to him. Never, that is, by word or deed, did he betray the truth to those of his fellow-clerks with whom he was intimate. All that he confided to one or two of his friends was that he loved, and was beloved by, a young lady of a superior class to his own, to whom he was engaged to be married.

In this dark story of secret passion and shame, yet another fact comes out clearly—namely, that

Madeleine Smith, on her side, soon became passionately devoted to her lover. To this fact hundreds of her letters testify, and in the long history of romantic love there is no more touching, no more pathetically human, correspondence than that of this girl of nineteen.

It is a one-sided correspondence, for only four letters written by Angelier to Madeleine survive, and, as we shall see, they are not kindly or pleasant epistles. But, though she destroyed his letters, he kept every scrap of her handwriting, including the artless note in which she wrote:

> I spent such a pleasant hour last evening reading your dear kind letters. I began with that little note which you gave to Bessie [her little sister]. I often thank God that you gave me that note, or 1 should not have known you. I love you with my whole heart and soul. Believe me, beloved of my soul, to be your devoted
>
> MIMI.

Angelier also kept—to his shame be it said —those of Madeleine's later letters which, according to the Lord Advocate, in his searching address at her trial, show "such an entire overthrow of the moral sense—the sense of moral delicacy and decency—as to create a picture which has never had its parallel in an inquiry of this sort."

But, in justice to Madeleine Smith, it must be plainly stated that this terrible verdict could only apply to very few of the letters—letters, be it remembered, which have been printed, not only in Great Britain and in America, but also translated into many languages.

The vast majority—the unhappy girl had the misery and the shame of hearing them all read aloud in court—are such as any passionately loving and pure woman might have written to the man she adored. Here is a typical example :

My Own, My Beloved Émile:

I write for you to get my note on your birthday. My beloved, may you have very, very many happy returns of the day—and each year may you find yourself happier and better than the last. I trust, darling, that on your next birthday I may be with you to wish you many happy returns in person. May you, dearest, have long life. My constant prayer shall be for your welfare and continued good health. I must conclude with a fond, fond embrace, a dear, sweet kiss. I wish it was to be given, not sent. Kindest, warmest love to you, my husband dear. Love again from thy very fond, thy loving, and ever devoted

Mimi,
Thy Own Wife.

In yet another long letter she thus alludes to their forthcoming marriage :

> Will we require to be married in Edinburgh, or will it do here? I fear that in Glasgow there are so many people who know me. But we must manage in some way to be united ere we leave town.
>
> How kind of Mary Perry to take trouble with us! She must be a dear, good creature. I shall never forget the first visit I paid with my own beloved husband to the dear darling.
>
> Sweet love, I adore you with my heart and soul. How are your mother and sister? Well, I hope, my own sweet.
>
> Much more love, kisses tender and longing. I am thy own, thy loving wife, thy
>
> MIMI ANGELIER.

As is well known, the marriage law in Scotland is very different from that of most civilized countries. The fact that a single man and woman have pledged each other as husband and wife, with the knowledge of third persons, may constitute a marriage. We cannot, therefore, wonder that Angelier, who knew that Madeleine had taken one of the servants in her father's house into her confidence, came to regard her as his wife by the law of Scotland, though it is doubtful whether a court of law would have held this association to be a valid " marriage by repute." But it is clear that Madeleine did not regard herself as his legal wife, in spite of her constant use of the word " wife " in her letters. This is proved by the following note, obviously written in answer to a jealous outburst on the lover's part:

My Own, My Beloved Husband:

Why do you say in your letter " If we are not married " ? Beloved, have you a doubt but that we shall be married some day?

My kind love to your dear sisters when you write. They shall be my sisters some day. I shall love them if they are like their brother, my dear husband. I know you have but little confidence in me ; but, dear, I shall not flirt—I shall only be pleasant to gentlemen. You must tell me at the end of the summer if you have heard anything about my flirting, and you will see how good your Mimi has been. Yes, I see you smile and say, " If she has a chance." Try and trust me—love me.

Beloved, adieu. God bless you and make you well, and may you yet be very, very happy with your Mimi as your little wife.

Kindest love, fond embrace and kisses from thine own true and devoted Mimi,

THY FAITHFUL WIFE.

In a postscript to another long letter she says :

True and constant shall I prove. Don't give ear to any report you may hear. There are several, I hear, going about regarding my going to get married.

Accept dear love, from thy devoted and loving, much attached wife,

THINE OWN MIMI.

I am thine till death do separate us.

Again, evidently in answer to some chiding word:

Beloved, Dearly Beloved Husband:

I am no longer a child, but be sure I shall be true and faithful wherever you are, dear love. Your income will be quite enough for me—don't for a moment fancy I want you to better your income. No, dearest ; I am quite content with the sum you make. When I first loved you I knew you were poor. I felt I would be content with your lot, however humble it might be ; with your home, in whatever place or whatever situation it is or will soon be. Never fear my friends and family will cast me off. If they did so, I should know they were not worth having. If they cast me off because we are poor, why, they will be much better away from us. If it is only for money that they love, their friendship is unworthy. I do not love you less because you are poor —no, I should love you even more, try to make you more comfortable, try to make you forget you are poor.

That her love was unselfish during those days is also made plain by the following :

> Émile, you made me a rash promise in your last letter. You said that though I was dead you would never marry again, and this you swore. Émile, that was wrong. You must promise me that if I should die you will marry, and that as soon as you can. Is not a man happier with a wife ? Is she not a happiness and a comfort to him, a solace in his sad hours, a help in his old age, a blessing to him if he has a family ? No, darling Émile, I do not want you to promise such a thing. I think every man, as soon as he has found his love, should take her to wife. And, darling Émile, never repeat again to me that life is a burden to you. You have a wife who loves you fondly, truly—loves you with a heart which burns with pure love for you, my only love. When you are sad, think of your
>
> MIMI.

Angelier seems to have wished to improve the girl he loved. He evidently scolded her and found fault with her frequently ; again and again we find Madeleine deferring to his wishes, and assuring him that she will follow his advice, and try to make herself perfect—for his sake :

> I am trying to break myself of all my very bad habits. It is you I have to thank for this, which I do sincerely from my heart.

But gradually, we feel as we read, a change in the tone of the girl's letters. " Yours with love and affection " takes the place of " Thy devoted, thy passionately loving wife "; and at last comes the first allusion to William Minnoch :

> I did tell you at one time that I did not like him ; but he is so pleasant that he has quite raised himself in my estimation.

And a little later, evidently in answer to a letter in which Angelier spoke jealously of the prosperous merchant :

> I wept for hours after I received your letter, and this day I have been sad—yes, very sad. My Émile, I love you, and you only. It was Minnoch that I was at the concert with—see, I do not hide it from you. Émile, he is papa's friend, and I know papa will have him at the house. But need you mind that, when I tell you that I have no regard for him ? I promise you I shall be seen as little in public with him as I can. I have avoided him at all times, but I could not on Wednesday night. So, sweet love, be reasonable.

But Angelier did not become reasonable, and Madeleine again put forth all her wit to soothe him and lull his suspicions :

> You ought not to believe any idle report. I know I talk to him—I could not sit still

without talking a whole evening; but I
did not flirt. There is a difference between
flirting and talking. He was not with me
last night.

And then, so strange and capricious is human
nature, suddenly she wrote a few lines as loving
as any she had ever written:

Forgive me for all I have done to vex
you, sweet love. I adore you with my heart
and soul. I would be happy if I could see
you for one hour. I am thy staunch, loving
wife, thine own dear, faithful, true, and
loving little wife, thy
MIMI ANGELIER.
P.S.—I do so like the " Mimi Angelier."
It is such a dear, pretty name. I love it so.
A kiss—another.

But, after this final burst of adoring affection,
once more the tone of Madeleine's letters cools;
they are still, in a sense, true, devoted, and
affectionate, but the tone completely alters:

I have never felt so restless and so unhappy as I have done for some time past.
A dark spot is in the future. What can it
be? Oh, God keep it from us! I weep now,
Émile, to think of our fate. Alas! Alas!
I see no chance, no chance of happiness
for me.

III

Angelier's jealousy grew and grew till it became a very upas tree, shadowing his love for the girl he named, in the one real love-letter of his which survives, " My beloved wife."

When the Smith family were in town, the lovers were able to meet only at night, and with considerable risk of discovery. Very early in the correspondence we find Madeleine firmly refusing to see Angelier, except when her father is obliged, by his work as an architect, to leave Glasgow for two or three days at a time. Then, and then only, did the girl consent, with a servant, Christina Haggart's, connivance, to admit her lover into the house. Even then, as can be imagined, their interviews were necessarily brief, and, to Madeleine, fraught with the dreadful knowledge that some trivial sound or disturbance might at any moment bring her mother downstairs to discover the shameful truth.

Often the lover had to content himself with a whispered conference at the beloved's heavily barred window, which was half sunk below the level of the street. Angelier used to slip his letters down, so that they rested on the sash of the window, and he put them, at Madeleine's suggestion, in brown envelopes, that they might escape notice during the hours that had to elapse before she could take them in unobserved.

One can imagine how intolerable grew such subterfuges to a sensitive, irritable man whose only wish was to make the girl he loved his wife.

And then, as was bound to happen, there came the fatal day when Angelier heard a rumour of Madeleine's actual engagement to William Minnoch. This drew from Angelier a stern epistle, of which, oddly enough, a press copy was found among the writer's effects :

Mimi :
There is a foundation for what I have heard. You often go to Mr. M's. house, and if you were not on the footing reported you could not do so.

Mimi, place yourself in my position. Show me if I am wrong in believing what I hear. I insist on having an *explicit* answer to the questions you evaded in my last letter. I must try and find some means of coming to the truth. I do not wish you to answer me at random. Answer me this, Mimi : who gave you the necklace you showed me? Was it Mr. Minnoch ? Is it true that you are, directly or indirectly, engaged to Mr. Minnoch, or to any one else but me ? These questions I must have answered.

May God bless you, pet, and with many fond and tender embraces,
    Believe me, with love,
        Your ever devoted husband,
            ÉMILE ANGELIER.

Madeleine *was* engaged to William Minnoch; the necklace in question *had* been given to her by him; and her betrothal to her father's friend was already being bruited about Glasgow. One wonders whether the following letter was in answer to Angelier's accusing and probing note, or whether other letters had passed between them in the meantime:

> *Émile:*
> I felt truly astonished to have my last letter returned to me. But it shall be the last you will have an opportunity of so returning. As there is coolness on both sides, our engagement had better be broken. This may astonish you, but you have more than once returned me my letters, and my mind is made up that I shall not stand the same thing again. Altogether, I think, owing to coolness and indifference (nothing else), we had better for the future consider ourselves as strangers. I trust to your honour as a gentleman that you will not reveal anything that may have passed between us. I shall feel obliged by your bringing me my letters and likeness on Thursday evening at seven. C. H. [the servant who had been their confidante] will take the parcel from you. I trust that you may be happy, and get one more worthy of you than am I.

And in a long postscript:

5

You may be astonished at this sudden change—but for some time you must have noticed a coolness in my notes. I did once love you fondly, but for some time back I have lost much of that. It is but fair to let you know this. It has cost me much to tell you. It is better that you should know. I know you will never injure the character of one you so fondly loved. No, Émile; I know you are honourable and a gentleman.

To this letter Angelier sent no reply, and the anxious girl wrote the next day :

I attribute it to your having a cold that I have had no answer to my last letter. I again appoint Thursday night, seven o'clock.

And then, at last, he seems to have answered, not only refusing to return her letters, but threatening to take these straight to her father. In reply to that awful threat there came this agonized plea for mercy :

Monday night.

Émile :

I have just had your note. Émile, for the love you once had for me, do nothing till I see you. For God's sake, do not bring your once loved Mimi to an open shame. Émile, write to no one, papa or any other. Oh, do not, till I see you on Wednesday night! It would break my mother's heart. I am the most guilty, miserable wretch on the face of the earth. When I ceased to love you, believe me, it was not to love another. Émile, for God's sake, do not send any letters to my papa. It will be an open rupture. I will leave the house. Do nothing till I see you. One word to-morrow night at my window, or I shall go mad. Émile, you did love me! I did fondly, truly love you too. Oh, dear Émile, be not so harsh to me! Oh, Émile, pray for me for a guilty wretch, but do nothing. Ten o'clock to-morrow night. One line, for the love of God!

Tuesday morning.

I am ill. God knows what I have suffered. My punishment is more than I can bear. Do nothing till I see you. For the love of heaven do nothing! I am mad —I am ill.

There is no doubt that an interview between the two did take place—in fact, the servant who had been in their confidence admitted as much. But during that interview Angelier, who had always shown himself a man of determined character, absolutely refused to return Madeleine's letters, or to abandon his intention of marrying her.

He plainly told her that he would not allow their engagement to be broken—rather than that should happen, he would place her letters in her father's hands ; and Mr. James Smith, once cognizant of the correspondence, would have no course open to him but to allow his daughter to become Angelier's wife.

It must have been just after this secret meeting that Madeleine, for the first time in her life, made an attempt to procure poison. She instructed her mother's page-boy to try and purchase some prussic acid, which she said she required as a cosmetic. But the boy was unsuccessful in his quest.

Again we have a despairing letter from her to Angelier, which, so urgent was her need, she sent by hand :

> *Émile :*
> I have this night received your note. No one can know the intense agony of mind I suffered last night and to-day. Émile, my father's wrath would kill me. You little know his temper. For the love you once had for me, do not denounce me to my papa. Émile, if he should read my letters to you, he will put me from him— he will loathe me as a guilty wretch. I loved you, and wrote to you in my first ardent love. It was with my deepest love I loved you. I put on paper what I should not. I did so because I loved you with all my heart. If he or any other one saw those fond letters to you, what would not be said of me ? On my bended knees I write to

you, and ask you, as you hope for mercy on the judgment day, not to inform on me. Do not make me a public shame. You may forgive me, but God never will. For God's love forgive me and betray me not. For the love you once had for me, do not bring down my father's wrath on me. It will kill my mother (who is not well). I am humbled before you, and crave your mercy. Will you not keep my secret from the world? Oh, do not, for Christ's sake, denounce me. Shame would be my lot. I did love you, and it was my soul's ambition to be your wife. I asked you to tell me my faults : you did so, and it made me cool toward you gradually.

And then comes the piteous and quite true statement :

Émile:
I have suffered much for you. I lost much of my father's confidence that September. [This was when their first innocent connection had been discovered.] And my mother has never been the same to me. No, she has never given me the same kind look. For the sake of my mother—her who gave me life—spare me from shame. Oh, Émile, will you, in God's name, hear my prayer? I have prayed that He might put in your heart yet to spare me from shame. I am humbled to thus crave your pardon. I blush to ask you.

Oh, for God's sake, for the love of heaven, hear me! I grow mad. I feel as if death would indeed be sweet. Denounce me not. Émile, Émile, think of our love. Pardon me; if you can, pray for me as the most wretched, guilty, miserable creature on the earth! I could stand anything but my father's hot displeasure. If he is to get these letters, I cannot see him any more. And my poor mother! I should never more kiss her. Émile, will you not spare me this? Hate me, despise me—but do not expose me. I cannot, cannot write more. I am too ill to-night.

M.

No word from another pen could paint as vividly as do these piteous letters Madeleine Smith's state of mind. She was, as we know, and as Émile Angelier suspected, actually engaged to William Minnoch. But, reading these agonized appeals, we feel that it was not of Mr. Minnoch whom she thought when inditing them—it was of herself, and of her relation to the father and mother she fondly loved.

Did Madeleine Smith, by Angelier's harshness, feel herself tempted to compass the death of the man whom she had once passionately loved?

To that question no certain answer can ever be given, for now we begin to enter a world, not of reality, but of conjecture.

The two certainly met again, but what took place at the interview will never be known. It is evident that the quarrel was so far composed —incredible as it now seems—as to allay and lull to rest Angelier's jealous fears of Minnoch. And once more we find Madeleine, in her letters to the young foreigner, adopting her old tone of affection.

But meanwhile her engagement to Mr. Minnoch was becoming more and more known in the town. She was receiving the congratulations of his friends and of hers ; he was daily giving her presents ; at last there came a day when the date of the wedding was fixed—and still Angelier kept securely in his possession the wretched girl's incriminating letters.

IV

And now the curtain rises on the final act in the drama.

Early in March, while dining with his friend, Miss Perry, Angelier casually informed her that he was to see Madeleine the following Thursday.

It was on that very Thursday night that he was seized with a sudden illness. He lay on the floor of his lodgings, so ill that he could not call assistance for some time ; and when at last his landlady came in answer to his cries and his moans, she thought that he would die.

At last, after much suffering, he grew better, and at the time those about him supposed that he had had a slight attack of the cholera then rife in Glasgow. *But the symptoms were also the symptoms of arsenical poisoning.* However, he recovered so completely that he was out on the following Saturday.

On the next Monday—not before, be it noted —Madeleine is known to have purchased some arsenic at the shop of the family chemist. She asked for the poison openly, saying that it was required to destroy rats in her father's country house.

Meanwhile, Angelier had been informed that he ought to have a change of air. Madeleine wrote:

> *Dearest, Sweet Émile:*
> I am sorry to hear you are ill. I hope to God you will soon be better. Do not go to the office this week. I have not felt very well these last few days—sick and headache. Every one is complaining; it must be something in the air! I shall not be at home on Saturday, but I shall try, sweet love, to write, even if it should be the smallest word. Do not come and walk about and become ill again. You did look bad Sunday night and Monday morning.

Miss Perry afterward asserted, in the witness-box, that just about this time Angelier and she held a singular conversation. He said his love for Madeleine was a fascination, and he used the strange expression, "If she were to poison me I would forgive her." And that was said, according to Miss Perry, in connection with the very serious statement that his illness had followed his taking a cup of coffee or cocoa from Madeleine's hand.

When Angelier was about to leave Glasgow for change of air, Madeleine made a determined effort to persuade the young man to go to England—she suggested the Isle of Wight. Angelier did not take her advice, and in one of the only four letters that were found in his handwriting he said:

My Dear, Sweet Pet Mimi:
You must not blame me for feeling hurt. Your letters are so shot, without a particler of love in them. And the manner you evade answering my questions fully convinces me that there is foundation in the talk of your marriage with another. I cannot travel five hundred miles to the Isle of Wight and five hundred miles back. The doctor says I must go to Bridge of Allan. What is your object in wishing me so very much to go south?

Those who later became her ardent advocates pointed out that Madeleine's object might have been to insure that Angelier should be far away

5*

when her marriage to Mr. Minnoch actually
took place. Once she had become Mrs. Minnoch,
it would have been the act of a vindictive
fiend—and Angelier was no fiend—to have
betrayed the correspondence to either father or
husband.

But Angelier, as we see, refused to go away,
and the unhappy Madeleine bought arsenic
again—this time while out walking with a girl
friend, and she signed the chemist's " poison
book " with her own name.

And now let us closely follow the doomed
man—doomed, whether he was indeed done
foully to death, or whether, as is just possible,
he took his own life.

Receiving leave of absence from his employers,
Angelier went to Edinburgh, where he saw some
friends. While in Edinburgh he is said to have
repeated the curious statement that he had been
given a cup of coffee by an acquaintance, and
that illness had immediately followed.

" I do not wonder so much that I should be ill
after cocoa, for I am not accustomed to it; but
that I should be ill after coffee, which I take
regularly, I can not account for," he is reported
to have remarked.

He then went back to Glasgow, and seemed
troubled to find no letter in his lodgings. He
stayed at home all one day, and then, at last,
he started for Bridge of Allan. After his

departure a letter did come, and was duly forwarded to him.

That letter was never found. Had it been found, it might have made all the difference to Madeleine Smith. Only the envelope was discovered, empty, in one of Angelier's pockets. He came back to Glasgow earlier than his landlady expected him, and it was there that he found yet another letter, which he did preserve, and which was put in as evidence at the trial:

> Why, my love, did you not come to me? Oh, beloved, are you ill? 'Come to me, sweet one. I waited and waited for you, but you came not. I will wait again to-morrow night, same hour, same arrangement. Come, beloved, and press me to your heart. A kiss, fond love. Adieu, with tender embraces. Ever believe me to be your own ever dear fond
>
> MIMI.

That letter, with the envelope of the other, was in the pocket of the dead man's coat; but no date was mentioned in the letter, and there was nothing to show which night the writer had meant by "to-morrow night."

On the Wednesday in that week Madeleine bought a third packet of arsenic, telling the chemist that more rats had been found in her father's country house. As Miss Smith had obtained arsenic before, and as she told her story without any hesitation, the poison was given to her.

On Thursday night Angelier left his lodgings, in his usual health, a little before nine o'clock. He was seen walking alone in the direction of Blythswood Square about twenty minutes past nine. But from that time onwards, he was as if obliterated from humankind for five hours.

There was a policeman whose duty it was to pace up and down in front of No. 7, Blythswood Square all night, and he most positively denied that anyone had lingered near the basement windows, or even approached the house, that night.

Between two and three in the morning Angelier came back to his lodgings in such pain that he even lacked strength to turn the latch-key.

He was doubled up with agony, speechless, parched with thirst, burning with fever. As the night went on he grew more and more ill; but while his kindly landlady was attending to his needs he said nothing as to where he had been, or as to what could have caused his illness.

When the woman proposed to send for a doctor, he refused to have one called. But at last, growing worse, he suddenly cried out: "If he is a good doctor, bring him!"

The doctor contented himself with sending a prescription, and the landlady, thoroughly frightened by her lodger's condition, asked:

"Is there no one you would like to see, Mr. Angelier?"

He replied feebly: "I should like to see Miss Perry."

Miss Perry was sent for, but before her arrival Émile Angelier was dead.

And then there happened the very thing which Madeleine Smith had dreaded with so great and piteous a dread. Angelier's body was scarcely cold before the letters she had written to him were discovered by one of his fellow-clerks, and within a very few hours the whole correspondence had been placed before the girl's horrified parents.

Meanwhile, a post-mortem held in haste revealed that Angelier had died from arsenical poisoning, and the police took charge of all the dead man's effects.

V

When Madeleine, after her arrest, was faced with the awful accusation of having compassed Angelier's death, her whole manner altered, and at once she assumed the attitude of one proudly conscious of innocence. Further, when closely interrogated by the magistrate, she spoke with a degree of candour and openness which greatly impressed him. She frankly admitted that she had expected to see Angelier at her window the previous *Saturday* night; but she asserted that he had disappointed her and that, as a matter of fact, she had not seen him for three weeks before his death.

Her statement was confirmed by the little sister who slept with her, and who declared most solemnly that Madeleine had not stirred during the Thursday night when Angelier met his death.

Questioned as to the arsenic she had bought, she confessed that she had lied as to the purpose for which she required it, her real intention being to use it as a cosmetic.

For two months Madeleine Smith lay in prison while the case against her was being prepared, and the excitement and interest roused by the affair increased daily, it might almost be said hourly. The whole English-speaking world of that day was divided into two camps—those who believed her innocent and those who believed her guilty. The latter asked why, if Madeleine Smith was innocent, did she leave her father's house secretly in the early morning after she had heard from Miss Perry's visit of Angelier's death? Those who were convinced that she was falsely accused declared that she had been driven to this incriminating flight by shame

NOT PROVEN : MADELEINE SMITH 121

at the thought that now, at last, her clandestine correspondence would be seen by her father and mother.

On the last day of the June following the March in which Angelier's death took place, the trial of Madeleine Smith opened amid a scene of the tensest excitement. The case had been transferred to Edinburgh, for it was not thought that a Glasgow jury could be impartial in a case so near their own doors. The Lord Justice Clerk, the head of the Scottish criminal judges, tried the case, assisted by two other judges. The greatest lawyers, the keenest forensic intellects of the day, were engaged either for the Crown or for the Defence; and, as the case proceeded, the excitement and suspense of Madeleine's advocates —and they were in the vast majority—grew almost unbearable.

It was said by an eye-witness that the prisoner stepped into the dock with "a step as buoyant, and with eyes as bright, as if she were entering a box at the opera." And when called upon to plead, she answered in a clear, sweet treble: "Not guilty."

The story that was then unfolded has been set out clearly in the preceding pages; but it may be noted that the defence relied mainly on the fact that there was no evidence at all to show that Madeleine had had arsenic in her possession *at the date of Angelier's first illness.* Every chemist in Scotland had been visited and questioned, but the investigation had yielded no result.

With regard to motive—the corner-stone in every murder trial—it was, of course, pointed out that no possible advantage could have accrued to Madeleine by Angelier's death, so long as her incriminating letters remained in existence, and in his possession.

Only twice during her nine days' ordeal did Madeleine Smith show the agitation and anxiety natural to the dreadful position in which she found herself.

The first time this occurred was when her one-time lover, William Minnoch, stood in the witness-box. He studiously avoided looking towards the dock; but the prisoner fixed her large blue eyes on him with an anguished expression while, in a low, pained voice, he told the story of their engagement, and read the rather prim little letters he had received from her.

The second occasion on which the unhappy girl broke down was when her ardent love-letters to Angelier were being read aloud in the monotonous voice of the clerk of the court.

During the long time the reading lasted she

hid her face in her hands, and her low, bitter sobs were audible throughout the whole of the packed court-house.

But when there came the terrible incriminating charge of the Lord Advocate, Madeleine's face did not move a muscle, and the pure fresh colour in her cheeks came and went as usual. She also appeared unmoved during the splendid and eloquent defence which followed. But the summing-up by the Lord Justice Clerk moved her to keen attention—and well might she attend, for it was his duty to hold the balance true and even before the fifteen men who were there to decide whether she should go free, or die a shameful death.

On the whole, it was thought that the Lord Justice Clerk leaned to the side of mercy. After going over the whole of the evidence as presented by the Crown, he laid stress on the fact that Angelier at various times in his earlier life had threatened, and that most seriously, to commit suicide. Best of all, from the point of view of those who loudly declared their belief in the prisoner's innocence, he ended by laying special stress on the fact that there was no evidence at all to show that Angelier on the night which preceded his death had been to Blythswood Square.

The jury retired. Madeleine, still composed, still with colour in her cheeks, was taken below.

Then slowly the jurymen filed back to their box, a great stillness fell on the court-house, and the foreman's voice rang out : " Not proven ! "

It is recorded that when the two fateful words were uttered the prisoner's face broke into a bright, nervous smile, and that only after receiving the warm hand-clasps of her able defenders did she shed tears.

At the time it was whispered that this verdict was due to the determined efforts of two jury-men, one of whom was convinced of the beautiful Madeleine's complete innocence of the charge, while the other put all his powers of persuasive eloquence to the task of convincing his fellows that, *if guilty*, she was justified in ridding the earth of so cruel and ungenerous a lover as Émile Angelier had shown himself to be !

And it was this last view which was generally endorsed by the public.

Madeleine Smith henceforth passed into the merciful shade of private life. But it may be added that she became, in time, the wife of a wealthy Englishman, and that she led, during many long years, the placid, happy existence of an exceptionally beloved wife and mother.

IV
MURDER FOR INSURANCE

MURDER FOR INSURANCE

THE DE LA POMMERAIS AFFAIR

I

WE first meet Edmond de la Pommerais at the age of twenty-four. He has just passed his last medical examination with brilliant success, greatly to the joy and gratification of his father (who is himself a well-known and highly respected country doctor) and of his doting mother.

The parents think it better that their only son should start practising in Paris, and so it is in Paris that we first make acquaintance with him.

Edmond de la Pommerais is exceptionally attractive. He is taller than the majority of Frenchmen, and he has a frank, open, kindly countenance. His father's well-to-do patients have given him excellent introductions in the capital, and he has everything that can make for happiness and repute.

The young doctor has been in Paris about three months when one day an old fellow-student

rushes into the pleasant bachelor rooms where
he has set up his household gods.

" I wish you would take over a case for me ! "
the visitor exclaims.　" I have to leave Paris
to-night—and this patient of mine is much to be
pitied.　His name is Louis de Pawr.　He and
his wife are both artists, and the wife is en-
chantingly pretty ! "

With his usual good nature, Edmond de la
Pommerais took over his friend's case, and went
to see the sick painter.　It is on record that
he behaved with extraordinary kindness and
generosity to this poor man, whom he found
already dying.　Nay, more, not content with
doing all he could for the artist himself, he
showed unbounded kindness to the latter's wife
and three children, and when Louis de Pawr
finally died, it was Dr. de la Pommerais who
paid part of the funeral expenses.

There then happened what doubtless has often
happened in such circumstances ; the young
physician went on seeing the pretty widow,
and soon they fell in love.

Séraphine de Pawr was considerably older
than Edmond de la Pommerais ; she was over
thirty, and according to French notions it was
out of the question that the two should marry.
They became, however, secret lovers, and during
the three years the intrigue lasted the doctor

paid the major part of the lady's expenses and those of her children.

But at last the young man grew weary of the irregular situation in which he found himself, and there came a day when, to the great anguish of Madame de Pawr, her lover bade her a solemn farewell.

For a while Edmond de la Pommerais devoted himself entirely to his profession. He was building up a good practice, and his family were busily engaged in trying to find him a suitable wife, when, one day, while in an omnibus, he noticed sitting opposite to him a very lovely girl, who was accompanied by her mother. So much attracted was he by her appearance that he followed the two ladies home. He discovered that their name was Dubisy, and, with some trouble, he obtained an introduction to them.

Very shortly after, La Pommerais declared his love for the girl, and asked her hand in marriage. Madame Dubisy, disapproving, as any French-woman of her type was certain to do, of so unconventional a way of contracting a matrimonial alliance, refused for some time to entertain the idea. But Mademoiselle Dubisy fell deeply in love with her romantic suitor, and in the end the mother gave way, and the young people were married amid the congratulations of all their friends, for Edmond de la Pommerais was known to be in receipt of a considerable income from his profession, and his bride had a good dowry.

However, the bridegroom was not so well off as he appeared to be. He gambled, as do so many Frenchmen, at cards; he also, which was far more serious, speculated on the Stock Exchange.

But he kept these worrying facts to himself, and in the brilliant Paris of the Second Empire there seemed no happier man than Edmond de la Pommerais.

Within two years of his marriage a daughter was born to the young couple, and a few days after the child's birth a kindly friend called.

" Why don't you have your baby insured ? " he said to the doctor. " By paying a small yearly premium, you will be able in ten or twelve years to provide yourself with a substantial sum of money to complete her education."

The father at once saw the good sense of the suggestion, and, after careful inquiry, sought out an insurance agent, and insured his baby girl.

Life then went on just as usual—outwardly prosperous and radiantly happy, inwardly cankered with secret money cares. These were temporarily relieved by the death of his wife's mother. That lady died rather suddenly while on a visit to the de la Pommerais, and she naturally left her property to her daughter; it came at a very convenient moment.

II

We now come to the second act of the drama, and we find ourselves this time in one of those tiny flats which form the apex of many old Paris houses. This particular flat contains only three rooms, and in it Séraphine de Pawr, now well over forty years of age, toils on at her profession of painting.

She is too poor to send her three children to school, and life becomes to her more and more a losing struggle with fate. Several years have gone by since she last heard of Edmond de la Pommerais, the good-looking, sunny-natured young man who gave her three such happy years; but she still cherishes a very tender feeling for him, and she cannot forget how kind he was, how generous, and, at one time, how absolutely devoted to herself.

Just now she is sitting by her wood fire, keeping it very low, for wood is dear, and she has no money coming in for two long days. But she has sent the children downstairs to a kindly neighbour whose kitchen fire is always burning.

Suddenly she turns round, and her care-worn face flushes, for she has heard a firm step on the staircase outside. There comes a ring at her door, and eagerly she goes to the door and opens it.

And then, to her incredulous joy, she sees that the man standing on the landing is none other than her one-time lover, Edmond de la Pommerais! Eagerly, tremblingly, she asks him to come in. "But don't take off your coat," she says solicitously, "for my sitting-room is so cold!"

But he strips off his comfortable fur-lined wrap, and takes both her thin hands in his.

"I mustn't make love to you," he says, smiling, "for I'm married now, Séraphine! But I thought that I would just come and see how you were getting on, and if there were anything I could do to help you."

Poor Séraphine, feeling as if she must be living through a happy dream, breaks down utterly, and bursts into tears.

Help her? Of course he can help her, though she hates to ask or to accept help from him! Never has she been in such terrible difficulty—the chief trouble being, of course, the children. If only she could afford to send them to the humblest day school! But she hasn't even enough to feed them, and, in addition, she is terribly anxious about the health of one of her little girls.

La Pommerais's professional instinct is aroused. "I will see the child," he says, "and I will do everything I can to cure her."

And then—for the mother, on hearing this,

goes and fetches her little girl from downstairs—
he proceeds to examine the child carefully,
tenderly, and kindly, and he does his best to
reassure the poor mother.

"All the child wants is good food, and you
can depend on me to see that she gets it."

Again he sits down, for, though he is a busy
man, he seems to be in no hurry that day.

Poor Séraphine, how happy she feels!—the
more so that her old friend questions her eagerly,
affectionately.

"How about your sister, Madame Ritter?"
he asks. "Does she not help you at all?"

Madame de Pawr shakes her head. "No; I
see very little of her now. You see, though
not so poor as I am, she is not in a position
to help me; so she hardly ever comes here
now."

"That's a great pity," he says, thoughtfully;
and then, drawing his chair close up to hers, he
whispers impressively, "Listen, Séraphine! I
have thought of a way in which I believe not
only your own future, but that of your children,
can be assured. But before telling you of my
scheme, I must warn you that it would be a
very serious thing both for you and for me if
you were to tell anyone anything about it, for
its success, as you will see, depends on our absolute secrecy."

"Is it likely that I should tell anyone our

secret ? " asks Madame de Pawr, proudly.   " Did
I ever speak of our former friendship ? "

" No," returns Dr. de la Pommerais, grate-
fully ; " I know I can trust you, and as you will
soon see I am going to do so.   And now I must
ask you to listen very carefully to what I am
going to say."

He gets up, goes to the door, opens it, sees
that there is no one on the landing, and then
sits down again.

" The first thing we must do is to insure your
life.   You are not much over forty, you are a
very healthy woman, and it will be comparatively easy to insure you for a large sum at a
reasonable rate."

Madame de Pawr looks at him, bewildered.

" But I haven't a penny in the world ! " she
cries.   " How could I possibly pay an insurance
premium ?   I only wish I could insure my life
even for only five thousand francs [£200] for the
children."

" Five thousand francs ? " echoes the young
man, laughing.   " That would be no good !   My
idea is to insure your life for five hundred
thousand francs [£20,000]."

Madame de Pawr stares at him, amazed indeed.

" And, what is more," he goes on, watching
to see how she is taking his extraordinary proposal, " I intend to pay the premiums myself !

I have been doing extremely well for the last two or three years, and I can afford it—the more so that the risk will not be for very long."

And then, as she looks at him with a queer feeling of misgiving—as well she may—he bursts out laughing.

" Oh, no ; I do not mean you are going to die ! " he says, gaily. " On the contrary, you have the kind of constitution that will help you to live to a hundred ! No, that's not what I mean at all ! "

And then Séraphine de Pawr's old friend and lover reveals to her a scheme, which, if fraudulent in intention, is yet most agreeably simple to carry out.

" After we have paid one or two premiums, you will have to simulate a serious illness—the sort of illness which means death within a short time."

" Yes," responds Séraphine, wonderingly.

" Now you will be bound, by the terms of your policy, to give notice to the insurance agent through whom it has been effected of your critical condition, and when he learns how ill you are the insurance office, alarmed at the thought of having to pay out so large a sum as five hundred thousand francs, will make you an offer of an annuity. I do not know exactly what offer will be made you ; that will, of course, depend on how ill they think you. But,

in any case, I do not think it can possibly be
less than a yearly income of four or five thousand francs—the more so that, with my help,
you will be able to appear *very* ill, while running
no real risk at all ! "

Were Madame de Pawr an honest woman,
she would, of course, reject this scheme ; but the
poor soul has had a terrible struggle ; she has
known what it is, not only to be hungry herself,
but to see her children hungry.   And then, an
insurance office !   She tells herself that an insurance office is like the Government !   No one
minds cheating the Government, so why should
one mind cheating a prosperous business concern
like a big insurance office ?

And so, foolish, trusting Séraphine accepts,
without a word of remonstrance, her one-time
lover's iniquitous proposal.   Nay, more ; on this,
his very first visit, she, at the doctor's dictation,
writes a letter to an insurance agent, whose name
and address he gives her, setting out that she
wishes to insure her life, and that the premiums
will be paid by a gentleman who has a direct
interest in the matter, as he is the father of her
three children.

Thus she not only consents to act with utter
want of honesty, but, further, she dishonours
herself and the memory of her husband in her
eagerness to give up her unequal struggle with
the wolf of want.

III

Strange to say, the business of insuring this poverty-stricken woman for the large sum of £20,000 was carried through with the greatest smoothness, secrecy, and simplicity. Edmond de la Pommerais did not personally appear in the matter at all. On the contrary, he took the very greatest care to remain outside the matter altogether, though he was, at last, obliged to allow his name to be quoted as guarantor, for the premium was nearly £800 a year.

Once the first premium had been paid, the policies were made out (for the risk was distributed among eight offices), and then the doctor applied the whole of his considerable intellect to the problem of how to secure the ultimate payment of the policies directly to himself. This was not easy, for he was anxious to keep quite clear of the whole business until the moment should come when the money would actually fall due.

He was aware, as we have seen, that Madame de Pawr had a sister better situated than she was herself.

How dreadful it would be if, when the insurance fell in, this sister were to come forward, claim the money, and invest it for the three young de Pawrs!

Accordingly he sought out a reputable

lawyer, whom he informed that he had at
various times lent a large sum of money to a
widow called de Pawr, in days gone by when
he was a very young man, and much in love
with the lady. He also told the lawyer that he
did not wish the fact to come out, as he was
now happily married to a wife to whom he was
devoted. Fortunately, so he went on to say, his
old friend, though she could not pay the money
back, was on friendly terms with him, and quite
willing to insure her life for the amount in question.

Dr. de la Pommerais did not inform his lawyer
that the sum was £20,000. He said the sum
was £4,000—and even that must have seemed
a very large amount for a young doctor to have
lent a poor widow.

Very odd money transactions do sometimes
take place between foolish young men and de-
signing women, and, taking the prosperous
doctor's word for what had happened, the lawyer
made out a deed transferring the policy of insurance to his client " in consideration of value
received."

De la Pommerais took the document home and
copied it exactly, the only difference being that
he substituted the words " 500,000 francs " for
" 100,000 francs."

As a further precaution, he asked Madame de
Pawr to make a will leaving him any money

which came to her under her insurances, in order
that he might look after her children, whom, he
said, he loved as he did his own little daughter.

Trusting Séraphine, blinded by her gratitude
—for to her the annuity she hoped to get from
the insurance offices seemed untold wealth—
assented to all he desired.

IV

Once more we find Madame de Pawr sitting
idly in her little cheerless sitting-room. But she
no longer looks anxious and careworn. She is
no longer unhappy and wretched, as she was
three or four months ago ; for she is receiving
each week a pension from her generous friend,
and, though he does not come very often, still he
comes from time to time to see her—and he has
cured her little girl.

And so, when she hears a step which has
become again a familiar, if not a frequent, sound
upon her stairs, she runs to the door and opens
it, with a happy smile.

" I have come to see you," says the doctor,
as he draws off his lemon-coloured kid gloves,
" because my wife is in the country, and I had a
spare hour. It has also occurred to me, my
friend, that the time has come when you had
better begin to pretend to be ill."

She laughs gaily. " It does seem rather soon,"

6

she says, cheerfully, " especially as I'm feeling
remarkably well ! "

" Yes ; but it's not too soon if our scheme is
to succeed. You will have to keep to your room,
and you must send for a doctor—it had better
be a complete stranger. As to the illness——"
he hesitates.

" Shall I pretend to have an accident on the
stairs ? " she suggests.   " You know how steep
they are ! "

And he nods gravely.

That same night the people in the house were
disturbed by a loud noise on the staircase, and
the next morning none of them were surprised
to learn that Madame de Pawr had had a bad
fall, and was obliged to keep to her room. As
she continued to feel far from well, a kindly
neighbour sent for the doctor she herself
always consulted. He naturally believed Séraphine's story, and treated her for shock, and for
a bruise which was non-existent.

But days lengthened into weeks, and Madame
de Pawr did not get any better. The doctor
attending her was puzzled, but, as all medical
practitioners are aware, a severe nervous shock
often takes mysterious forms.

At last someone seems to have told Madame
de Pawr's sister of her illness, so the next visitor
we see in the little flat is Madame Ritter.

" What is this I hear about your having had an accident ? " she asks, anxiously. " It's very odd, because you look so extremely well."

" Do I ? " Madame de Pawr laughs, mysteriously. " Well, I'm not perhaps quite as ill as I appear to be ! "

" What can I do for you, my dear ? " says the other. " I haven't got much money, as you know, but I would very much rather do without something myself than see you ill and miserable."

Séraphine is touched by her sister's solicitude. " I wonder if you could really keep a secret," she whispers, hesitatingly.

" Of course, I should never dream of repeating anything you told me ! " cries Madame Ritter.

And then Madame de Pawr, careless of her solemn promise to Edmond de la Pommerais, repeats to her sister, word for word, the proposal made by him, and boasts of their joint success in carrying it out.

Strange to say, Madame Ritter expressed no surprise or horror at what was being done, but went away promising to keep secret the plan which these two people had made to cheat the eight insurance companies.

V

We are now at the beginning of the last act of the sombre drama.

Madame de Pawr had already been in bed a month, and she was beginning to look seriously ill from the confinement and the unhealthy life she was leading, when Edmond de la Pommerais came to see her.

" I think the time has come," he observed, " to inform the insurance agent that you are ill. Now it is very probable that he will send one of the insurance companies' doctors to examine into your condition, and it won't do for whoever comes to find you as well as you are now. I propose therefore to give you a drug which will make you seem very ill—in fact, which *will* make you very ill—for a little while. But the bad effects will pass away in about twenty-four hours, and during that time you must bear the discomfort of feeling dreadfully sick and queer."

Madame de Pawr willingly assented.

She informed the insurance agent of her illness, and proceeded to take the " medicine " the doctor had sent her.

But the agent was quite content with the name of the respectable practitioner who was attending her regularly. Though she did not know it, and never was to know it, insurance offices never do engage medical men of their own to see those of their insured who are ill ; it would arouse the deepest resentment among the insured were they to do such a thing.

But poor Séraphine de Pawr longed for a visit

from the insurance companies' doctor, for she was really very ill, and it seemed a pity to go through all the pain and distress she was now suffering for nothing.

At last she was cheered by a note from La Pommerais saying that he was coming to spend the evening with her.

So overjoyed was she at the thought of seeing him in this pleasant, intimate fashion—for it was years since he had last spent an evening with her —that she actually sent out a neighbour to purchase some rouge, in order that she might look her best while her one-time lover honoured her by dining with her.

It is on record that Edmond de la Pommerais came at six that evening and stayed till about ten. No one saw him in the flat, but he was met coming there and seen going away.

That same night Madame de Pawr became terribly ill—so ill, indeed, that her children, terrified at her state, ran and fetched, not only some of their neighbours, but also their aunt, Madame Ritter.

But the unfortunate Séraphine de Pawr, if not a good woman, was a brave woman. She was ill—ill to death ; but she would not complain.

" Never mind ! " she kept whispering in trembling accents to her sister. " Remember that this is the price I am paying for my annuity of four or five thousand francs. Think of all I shall

be able to do with such an income ! Think of
the education I shall be able to give my darling
little girls. I mustn't mind a little pain, a little
discomfort, now."

Was there ever so pathetic, so ironical, so
horrible a situation as that of this brave, mis-
guided woman, dying, all unknowingly, by her
own hand ?

The long day wore itself away, and Séraphine
did not seem to get any better. The kind
neighbour once more went to her own doctor
and begged him to come at once ; but she had
foolishly told him that she had seen Madame de
Pawr pour away the medicine he had given her !
Naturally, much angered and disgusted by this
revelation of what he took to be his ungrateful
patient's stupidity and folly, the doctor refused
to attend her again.

" There's nothing the matter with her," he said,
impatiently. " She's an hysterical, silly woman,
and has simply got into the way of lying in bed
since her accident."

In the course of the evening Edmond de la
Pommerais came to see his suffering victim. He
seemed much concerned at her condition, and
gave her some more medicine. Then he went
away, mentioning the fact that he had to join his
wife, who was in the country near Paris.

Madame de Pawr grew worse and worse. But
she still kept up her spirits, and would not allow

what she called a " fuss " to be made. At last, however, she felt so terribly ill, and the griping pains became so intense, that she consented, rather unwillingly, that yet another doctor should be sent for by her neighbour.

When he came, this physician—who, of course, knew absolutely nothing about the case or her circumstances—at once declared that she had all the symptoms of cholera. He therefore gave her some drug which is supposed to relieve that awful disease—generally, be it remembered, endemic in Paris during the summer and autumn months—and went away.

The doomed woman—laughing even in the midst of her agony—told her eldest daughter that she did not think the new doctor's medicine would do her any good. But so serious had her state appeared to him that he came the next morning. By this time she was easier, but in a state of collapse, and about thirty hours after that little dinner for which she had tried to make herself exceptionally pretty and attractive, Séraphine de Pawr lay dead.

Toward evening of the same day, her one-time lover's young and vigorous step was again heard on the humble staircase.

The sad news was broken to him, and, with his arms round the three motherless children, he went and gazed at the corpse of the woman he had once passionately loved.

As he turned and left the room, he said to the neighbour who was taking charge of the children, " There seems no doubt that poor Madame de Pawr died of cholera " ; and the new doctor who had attended her during the last hours of her life signed the certificate, giving cholera as the cause of death.

The same night Edmond dela Pommerais wrote to the insurance agent, apprising him of the fact of Madame de Pawr's sudden death by cholera, and asking him to inform the eight insurance offices that the money due must be paid over to the writer, as he had a deed in his possession showing that the dead woman had transferred her interest in the insurance policies to him. He explained that it was the repayment of a large debt.

For a while everything fell out exactly as de la Pommerais had hoped it would do. His claim was duly acknowledged by the in-surance companies, and at poor Séraphine's funeral Madame Ritter thanked him for his goodness to her sister. But to her he did not say one word of his former loans to Madame de Pawr, or of the means which had been taken to pay him back.

The sum of £20,000 was just about to be paid over by the insurance companies, when the head of the Paris police received an anonymous letter, pointing out that there was something

strange about Madame de Pawr's death, and
that it would perhaps be worth while to ascertain who had had a pecuniary interest in the
event.

VI

It is now about a fortnight after the death of
Madame de Pawr. Edmond de la Pommerais
has not yet received the money due to him
under the deed of transfer, but various courteous
letters have passed between him and the insurance companies concerning the delay, and he is
expecting the money in a few days.

He is sitting at table with his young wife,
when there comes a sudden ring at the door.
Madame de la Pommerais glances across at
her husband. She has noticed that during the
last few days he has seemed a little nervous
when the bell rings—rather as if he were expecting an unwelcome visitor.

The maid comes in. " A gentleman to see
monsieur."

Edmond de la Pommerais takes the card, sees
on it a name unknown to him, but under the
name are the ominous words, " de la Sûreté."

He gets up from the table. " I shall not be
more than a few moments, darling," he says;
and we can picture with what a sick feeling of
dread he goes into his luxurious consulting-room.

For a moment he breathes more freely; before

6*

him stands a pleasant, smooth-faced official, who bows politely as the doctor comes in.

" Yes ? " says La Pommerais, inquiringly.

" I have come to see you, doctor," says the visitor, deferentially, " about a one-time patient of yours, a Madame de Pawr."

And then the young physician, still behaving as if the matter really concerns him very little, learns that the police, guided by an anonymous letter, have been making investigations. In fact, the woman's body has already been exhumed, and it is now known that very shortly before her death someone must have administered to her an enormous quantity of the vegetable poison known as digitalis—a poison which disappears from the body within a comparatively short time.

Certain papers have also been found in her flat which prove that she was very heavily insured, and the insurance companies, when approached by the police, state that Dr. de la Pommerais is the owner of the policies. That is why the Prefect of Police has sent a representative to ask the doctor how it came about that a woman as poor as Madame de Pawr should have been insured for so large a sum as £20,000. The police would also like to know where she procured the money, three months ago, to pay the first premium.

Edmond de la Pommerais—who, fortunately

for himself, has a very frank, pleasant manner—
at once takes the police official apparently into
his entire confidence.

" I will tell you all about it," he says, calmly,
and then he relates at length his carefully prepared story. But he so far modifies what he
probably intended to say that he now explains
that Madame de Pawr owed him only 20,000
francs ; and that the balance of the money is
going to be spent by him as trustee for her
children.

Then, going to a secret cabinet, he takes from
it the love-letters the unfortunate woman wrote
to him many years ago. He also fetches later
letters of hers, proving the debt, though in no
letter is the actual sum mentioned—indeed, these
pathetic epistles simply contain vague expressions
of gratitude for money received.

The police official listens courteously to the
long story. He takes leave of the doctor, but
the latter, on going to his window, sees that
there are detectives posted in the street below.

It is terrible to think of what the wretched
man must have gone through immediately after
the departure of his unwelcome visitor. He had
to tell his wife much the same story he had told
the police official ; the poor young woman learned
all at once of her husband's former intimacy with
Madame de Pawr, of his "follies " on her behalf,

of his imprudent renewal of their friendship, and last—though to her it seemed at the time least —of the preposterous half-accusation of murder with which he was now confronted.

Madame de la Pommerais, who was only twenty-one when this awful blow fell on her, behaved with wonderful magnanimity and trustful love. She accepted, unquestioningly, her husband's account of all that had taken place, and never admitted for a moment the theory of his guilt.

VII

The arrest of Edmond de la Pommerais quickly followed, and his old parents hastened to his aid. His father sought out Maître Lachaud, and engaged him to conduct his only son's defence.

Doubtless owing to the fact that the prosecution had to rely almost entirely on circumstantial evidence, as also to the social status of the accused, the trial aroused extraordinary interest in Paris, and, indeed, throughout all France.

An intimate friend of the Empress Eugénie was one of the young doctor's patients, and a firm believer in his innocence. It was whispered that, even if the prisoner were condemned, the Emperor would commute his sentence to lifelong imprisonment.

Meanwhile the prosecution, when probing into the doctor's past, had learnt of the sudden death of Madame de la Pommerais's mother. It had followed within a few hours of a meal taken in her son-in-law's house and company, and though no proof could be adduced, it was decided by the Public Prosecutor that the prisoner should be tried for the murder of his mother-in-law as well as of Madame de Pawr.

The trial,—which took place in the splendid old Palais de Justice, the destruction of which was to be perhaps the worst and most meaningless act of incendiarism committed by the Commune,—was the most noted *cause célèbre* of the Second Empire. Many of the Imperial Court officials were present, and from the first it was evident that popular sympathy was with the prisoner.

Madame de la Pommerais elected to be present in court the whole time, and her courage and self-command never left her, though much of the evidence tendered must have caused her the most acute anguish.

The chief witness for the prosecution was Madame Ritter. Word for word she repeated the long conversation she had held with her dead sister. The fact that the story she had come to tell was so much to her own discredit naturally vouched for its substantial accuracy.

Then came the evidence of the doctor who

had conducted the post-mortem, and who had discovered the digitalis in Séraphine de Pawr's remains.

The defence was able to call a long and distinguished list of well-known Parisians, who one and all testified to the prisoner's high personal and professional character.

Even more impressive was the appearance in the witness-box of some of the prisoner's humbler patients. They wept as they told of his generosity and unfailing care and kindness.

The mysterious death of Madame de la Pommerais's mother, a death which had proved so convenient in view of the doctor's financial embarrassments, was discussed at great length. This accusation rested on a structure composed partly of suspicion, partly of probability ; of proof there was none.

At last came the last day of the trial and the speech for the defence.

It will be remembered that Lachaud's first great oration in defence of a prisoner accused of murder had been delivered on behalf of Marie Lafarge, but the defence of the subtle de la Pommerais was a much more difficult task.

It is curious to compare the two cases. When he defended Madame Lafarge, Lachaud was young, inexperienced, full of contained passion, and convinced of his client's innocence. When he rose to make out the best case he could for de la

Pommerais, he was not only the greatest, but also the most fashionable, legal advocate in Imperial France. It was whispered that the Empress Eugénie had sent for him and begged him to do his best for the man she persisted in believing to be falsely accused of a vile crime.

The Public Prosecutor, Oscar de Vallée, had made a very moderate speech. One felt—so someone who was in court told the present writer—that in spite of his conviction of the prisoner's guilt he would have liked to save from the guillotine the fine young man now standing, quiet, composed, apparently unmoved, in the dock.

Thus Lachaud had had little to fear from his opponent. What he had to fear—and no one could have realized this better than himself—were inexorable facts.

Instead of trying to belittle these, as one less skilful might have done, he put his whole mind to drawing an attractive and touching picture of his client. He showed La Pommerais as a kind-hearted, generous physician, more assiduous and more attentive in his attendance on his poor than on his wealthy patients, and he quoted the many witnesses who had borne testimony to that fact. He gave a charming sketch of the way the popular young doctor had fallen in love at first sight with a girl whose modest fortune was the least of her attractions, and then he went on to describe their ideal married life, and the horrible, present anguish of the wife.

As he was fully entitled to do, Maître Lachaud went on to make great play with the fact that the Public Prosecutor had failed to establish that La Pommerais's mother-in-law had died from poisoning. In fact, those who heard the speech might have thought that that was the only, or at any rate the chief, accusation which had been brought against the prisoner.

But at last Maître Lachaud found himself compelled to attack what was, after all, the real matter in hand—the death of Madame de Pawr. Then, and not till then, were the judge and jury initiated into what is called in France the " system " of the defence.

It consisted in an attempt to prove that the prisoner in his bachelor days had in very truth given large sums of money to the widow, and that after the birth of his child he had felt it his duty to try and recover that money by any means, fair or foul, open to him.

Lachaud admitted that his client had been dishonest, that he had wished to cheat the insurance companies, partly with a view to providing for his ex-mistress, partly with a view to being repaid a portion of all that he had given her in the days of their liaison. He then analysed, with extraordinary skill, all the gossip and talk which had gathered round the story of

Madame de Pawr's death, and he proved that the woman had been in a very bad state of health even before she began the grim comedy which ended in her death. Finally, the great advocate wound up his very long and eloquent speech with the words :

"The murder has not been *proved*. It is impossible that you, gentlemen, will load your consciences with a verdict you might live to regret bitterly. This man was not an honest man, but that fact does not make him a murderer. The prosecution cannot even bring forward an atom of proof that he ever brought, still less that he administered, the poison to Madame de Pawr."

The speech made so considerable an impression on the judge that he had two of the medical experts recalled. But the jury, though they acquitted La Pommerais of having poisoned his mother-in-law, found him guilty *without extenuating circumstances* on the second count.

Edmond de la Pommerais was condemned to death mainly on the clear, pitiless evidence of Madame de Pawr's sister, Madame Ritter, who had forced herself to repeat in the witness-box, almost word for word, the imprudent confidences her sister had made to her.

To the last the Empress Eugénie believed in the young doctor's innocence. She discussed the case exhaustively with Lachaud; she even received in private audience the despairing wife ; and she persuaded the Emperor that, innocent or guilty, Edmond de la Pommerais had been condemned on purely circumstantial evidence.

It was whispered at the time that the document commuting the death sentence was already signed, when the high legal officers of the Crown one and all declared that they would resign if the Emperor interfered with the course of justice !

Be that as it may, Séraphine de Pawr's one-time lover was made to pay the full penalty of his crime.

To use an expression dear to criminals, Edmond de la Pommerais " died game." His last action on the scaffold was to hand the attendant priest a lock of his hair for his wife and child. And, as he was being strapped under the guillotine, he called out in a strong voice :

" Tell my parents, tell my beloved wife and child, that I die innocent—the victim of a judicial error."

V

WHO KILLED MR. BRAVO?

WHO KILLED MR. BRAVO?

I

My dear Charlie,

After serious and deep consideration, I have come to the conclusion that, if you *still hope* and wish to gain my love, we must see more of each other and be quite sure that the solemn act of marriage will be for the happiness of both. All I can *say* is that you have behaved in the noblest manner, and that *I* have no doubt of being happy with you ; but of course, before giving up my present freedom, I must be quite convinced it would be for our mutual happiness.

Need I tell you that I have written to the *Dr.* to say *I must* never see his face again ; it is *the* right thing to do in every respect, whatever happens, whether we marry or whether we do not. I shall ever have a great regard for you, and take a deep interest in your welfare, for I think you are a very good man. Write and tell me what you think of this letter, and with every kind wish,

Ever your sincere friend,
FLORENCE RICARDO.

P.S.—Of course this is sacred.

In answer to this, Charles Bravo wrote:

> *My dear Florence,*
> You are quite right. I approve thoroughly of what you say and do; and I may tell you that I am in danger of losing my chief jewel, my modesty, when I consider that you, whose opinion I most value, give me such high praise.

We must acknowledge that the high praise was justified, although to act generously and even nobly to a lovely young woman with whom one is passionately in love is no hard matter. So at least Charles Bravo found, when Mrs. Ricardo confessed, with sobs and tears, that since the death of her first husband she had had a lover in the person of a married man.

She further imprudently revealed the fact that the man in question was a certain Dr. Gully, who, long before the Bravo case was to make him notorious, was known to a large number of people as one of the most popular of provincial physicians, and also as a man possessing an extraordinary—many said an uncanny—attraction for women. The strength of this attraction is abundantly demonstrated by the fact that Dr. Gully, at the time of Mrs. Ricardo's infatuation for him, was sixty years of age, while she was still in her early twenties, and, in addition to her extreme loveliness, possessed a pleading charm

of manner and a winning sweetness of disposition which must have made her almost
irresistible.

The emotional life of every civilized Don Juan
is strewn with human wreckage, and they themselves as well as their victims often pay dearly
for their fleeting joys. But this one case must
have seemed to Dr. Gully the pleasant exception which sometimes comes to prove the
rule.

At the time of the secret intrigue, Mrs.
Ricardo was a wealthy widow, owing no duty
but to herself. Dr. Gully had retired from
practice full of years and honour, and was well-to-
do. Thus they were able to surround their
friendship with all necessary precautions and
safeguards. The lady's reputation did not
suffer, and her lover must have felt that, akin
to the fortunate hero of the cynical old verses :—

> On firmer ties his joys depend,
> He has a polished female friend.

True, Florence's own family were uneasy at
their daughter's intimacy with a married man.
Her mother implored her, again and again, to
give up her acquaintance with the doctor; and
when she would not do so, refused for a while
to see her.

But before Dr. Gully had tired of his con-
quest, the charming widow tired of him—or

perhaps it would be more true to say that she felt the separation from her mother, and that she grew weary of the ambiguous position into which she had drifted. Be that as it may, there came a day when she told her lover that their intimacy must cease, and that they must meet no more.

Dr. Gully sadly acquiesced, and though they went on living in the same neighbourhood—in fact, within a few hundred yards of one another—they no longer met, even as ordinary acquaintances.

Only one person in the world knew the whole truth as to their past relationship. This person was a certain Mrs. Cox, Florence Ricardo's paid companion and intimate friend.

Mrs. Cox? For more than three weeks all England rang with her name, and all England discussed, under its breath, her sinister, enigmatical personality. For this faded-looking, quiet, sensible-spoken widow was destined, whatever the truth, to play a remarkable part in the drama of love, of jealousy, and of death which makes the Bravo case one of the strangest and most mysterious in the annals of crime.

But to return to the days when Florence Ricardo was still free, still happy, still singularly enviable.

About the time she finally broke with Dr. Gully, the lovely widow became acquainted with

Charles Bravo. He was a good-looking, clever
young barrister, an Oxford man, the only son of
a doting mother, whose second husband was so
warmly attached to him that he meant to make
him his heir, and had insisted on his legally adopting his name.

Mr. Bravo straightway fell violently in love
with the charming widow, and offered her
marriage. Mrs. Ricardo had become accustomed to her freedom, but love begets love, and
she soon felt strongly attracted by Bravo's youth,
high spirits, and devotion to herself.

It is at this psychological moment that Mrs.
Cox emerges, for the first time, out of the shadow
in which she dwelt as trusted companion of the
wealthy widow.

Mrs. Cox found it quite easy to answer the
difficult question—" Should a woman tell ? "
She urged Mrs. Ricardo to confess to Charles
Bravo the truth as to Dr. Gully. She did even
more. After Florence had told Mr. Bravo her
painful secret and he had " forgiven " her, Mrs.
Cox actually tried to make the young man reveal
his future wife's past shame to his own mother,
who from the first had objected to the marriage,
and who was, perhaps naturally, jealous of the
beautiful and charming creature who had bewitched her son.

Whatever may have happened to be Mrs. Cox's
motive in urging Florence's lover to tell his

mother of his future wife's lapse, she met with unexpected opposition.

Charles Bravo was headstrong, foolish, impatient, but he was a gentleman—a man of honour. Touched to the heart by the confidence shown him by the woman he loved, he very properly determined that no one, least of all his mother, should ever share his painful knowledge. He went further; he solemnly promised Florence that the subject should never be mentioned between them.

At last, with the full assent of their respective families, Charles Bravo and Mrs. Ricardo became engaged, and their wedding day was fixed. Mrs. Cox's friend and employer refused to give her up, and it was settled that the companion should remain in the Bravo establishment as housekeeper to the married pair.

When one of the young lawyer's friends expressed some surprise that he cared to have a third person living with his wife and himself, he answered eagerly: " She will be very useful in supervising the servants. My wife is fond of her, and I owe Mrs. Cox something because she used to urge my suit."

So deeply, so passionately, was Charles Bravo in love, that he consented to what few Englishmen of his standing and independent fortune would have done. He agreed that they should stay on in The Priory, Balham, where his bride

had spent most of her widowhood, and that
though he knew her ex-lover, Dr. Gully, was
living within but a short walk of The Priory.

II

And then began what should have proved the
most prosperous and cloudless of married lives.

Charles Bravo and his bride were both young,
healthy, intelligent, and blessed with plenty of
money, for their joint income was not far short of
five thousand a year.

Bravo was a man of high animal spirits, who
could easily see the ludicrous side of things, as
is shown by his correspondence with his mother
and his stepfather. For instance, in a letter to his
mother he declares that by the orders of his
"better half" he has been obliged to wear "a
red flannel garment which is a cross between a
kilt, a sporran, and a pair of bathing-drawers,
and has as many strings as a harp."

At the same time, the intensity of his love for
his "better half" is shown in the letters he wrote
to her during the few absences which either was
compelled to make in the first year of their
married life. For example:

My own darling wife,
    I have been thinking all the morning of
the sweet girl I left behind me. Although

I passed the day in the fresh air, I was not happy; neither shall I be till I regain you. You will find me the best of husbands.

Again:

My darling Florence,
My poor mother is glad to have me back with her, and I am sure, if you hear the kind way in which she speaks of you, you would not mind my being with her. I cannot be happy in the absence of my best of wives. My only object in life is to make your life happy, and I hope I am succeeding.

In yet another letter he speaks of his feeling for her as " an exceeding great love."

But doubtless just because of his doting affection, Charles Bravo, very soon after his marriage, became seized with an agonizing, an intolerable, jealousy of his wife's past—not, be it remarked, of her past with Captain Ricardo, the good-looking, brilliant officer in the Guards, to whom she had been married in earliest youth, and to whom she had given all her heart, only to be treated—if we are to believe her own account— with neglect and indifference. To Ricardo, Bravo never seems to have given a thought. Instead, he concentrated all the jealousy, which soon became a bitter hatred, on the elderly physician with whom he was not even acquainted by sight, but whom he unfortunately knew to be still living close by.

When Charles Bravo rode past Dr. Gully's house, his horse used to tremble and break into a sweat—for horses, as all horse-lovers know, respond in an extraordinary degree to the sensations and the nerves of their riders. The young barrister, unlike many men, was quite incapable of controlling or hiding his feelings, and very soon he took to taunting his unfortunate wife with the secret he had solemnly promised to forget.

George Meredith's famous aphorism, "Men may have rounded Seraglio Point, they have not yet doubled Cape Turk," is only too true. Of human passions there is none so distressing, so disintegrating, it might almost be said, so fatal in its influence on human character, as jealousy, and especially is this the case with the jealousy of a man for a woman.

In vain poor Florence reminded her husband—the husband who was also, be it remembered, her cherished lover—that she had broken with Dr. Gully deliberately and of her own free will. In vain she reminded him of how sad and lonely a life she had been living after the death of her first husband—at the time, that is, when she had first fallen under Gully's spell. Nothing availed her. The fonder Charles grew of his wife—and he seems to have grown more fond, more uxorious, as the months went on—the more jealous he became of her past affection for their neighbour.

Small wonder that Florence Bravo began to droop, to become really ill, so ill indeed that she was ordered a change of air.

As always happens in such cases, Charles Bravo occasionally felt a pang of remorse for his unkindness and lack of generosity ; and in this connection we are able to quote a curious letter :

My darling Wife,
I know you to be the best of wives. We have had bitter trouble, but I trust that henceforth the sweet peace of our lives will not be interrupted. I feel that many of my words to you, although kindly meant, are perhaps unnecessarily harsh. In future my rebukes, if it should be necessary to say anything, which God forbid, shall be given with the utmost gentleness. I wish I could sleep away my life till you return. Come back as well as you can to your devoted husband.

I miss you, my darling wife, dreadfully. When you are back I will so take care of you that you will never leave me again. I walked up and down the road for half an hour waiting for a letter from you, and the postman came whistling along, the light-hearted wretch, although he had no letter for me !

But though, as the first year of their joint lives wore itself away, Mr. Bravo became, as was inevitable, more the affectionate husband and less the adoring lover, his jealousy suffered no abatement; it remained as fierce, as watchful, as suspicious, as ever. He habitually called Dr. Gully "that wretch." And when he was in a certain mood—the mood that every jealous husband knows—he would force his unfortunate wife to go and walk up and down in front of the other man's house. There he would ask, " Do you see anybody ? " She would answer, " No—I have not looked." And then they would walk home ; Florence feeling miserable and humiliated, Charles at once ashamed and angry because of his lack of self-control.

Occasionally Charles Bravo would utter vague threats. " I feel as if I could go and hang myself," he would say, " when I think of that wretch and you." And then again : " Wait, and you will see what I do when I get home." Then suddenly he would ask his wife to kiss him, " to make it up," and he would confess that no man in the world had ever had a sweeter and a kinder wife than he had in his Florence.

Together with his jealousy, there also came out another unpleasant, and, to a wife, a most trying, streak in Bravo's character. He began to show himself exceedingly " close " about money—indeed, money seems to have been never far absent from his thoughts. Even in one of his love letters we find the odd remark :

I miss you dreadfully. I would willingly give a hundred pounds—if times were not so hard—to have you here now !

" If times were not so hard " ? Times were not at all hard with this fortunate young man. He used to worry himself quite needlessly over the amount of money spent on the house-keeping. In vain did his wife remind him that she had always lived well within her ample income. He was ever trying to make her save, and he complained even of her purchasing small presents for her friends.

The young pair lived very comfortably. They had a big, roomy house, a number of servants who had been with Mrs. Ricardo for some years, and, as they were both fond of horses, they had, considering the way they lived, a rather large stable.

At last there came a day when Charles Bravo actually wrote to his wife : " By giving up the cobs and Mrs. Cox, we could save four hundred a year, and be as comfortable." But he added, as if a little ashamed of these words, " I only want your love. Without your love, riches and honours would be as nothing."

Mr. Bravo, however, had a more potent reason

than that of wishing to save money, for seeking to get rid of Mrs. Cox's perpetual presence in his house. He knew that she was aware of his wife's past, and also that she was cognisant of his present bitter jealousy of that past. But he found it very difficult to dislodge the tactful lady-companion from the comfortable home which had been hers so long. There was some talk of Mrs. Cox going to the West Indies, where she had certain business interests ; and Charles Bravo's stepfather even offered to pay her passage, but she refused.

Everything, indeed, was going on as usual at The Priory, when suddenly there occurred the tragedy of which the cause still remains an unsolved mystery.

III

Let us visualize as clearly as may be the strange sequence of events which took place on what Mrs. Bravo afterwards so truly called "the fatal Tuesday."

It was a fine, early spring day, and Charles Bravo, still so devoted to his wife as to wish to have her with him on all occasions and for as long as possible, persuaded Florence to drive him to his chambers.

On the way there burst out what had unfortunately become one of their usual quarrels, and that morning it seems to have been more bitter, more painful than usual. Not only did Mr. Bravo abuse Dr. Gully, but he went so far as to say, " I shall never get over it ! I sometimes think we had better separate ! "

His wife was cut to the heart by these words. She reminded him that she did everything to make him happy, and she recalled his own suggestion, nay, his solemn promise, that the curtain over the dark corner of her past life should never be lifted.

Her tearful words must have moved him, for suddenly he exclaimed that he knew he was wrong, and earnestly he asked her to kiss him as a token of her forgiveness. She refused to do so, and he said, " If you do not kiss me, you will see what I will do when I get home ! "

And then the poor woman did kiss him, and they were reconciled.

Florence drove back alone to The Priory, and told all that had taken place to Mrs. Cox.

Meanwhile Bravo lunched with a friend—he was a man with hosts of friends—who thought him in the best of health and spirits, and in the early afternoon he went home. As was his frequent custom, he went out for a ride on one of his wife's cobs ; it bolted with him, and when back at The Priory he complained of feeling shaken and tired by the unpleasant experience.

Though Charles Bravo was still suffering

from the accident he had had out riding, and though Florence was still sufficiently of an invalid to go straight to bed after her evening meal, they both dressed for dinner, as did also Mrs. Cox. They had the customary soup, fish, an entrée, roast meat, pudding, and, in the way of wines, sherry for the ladies, and for Mr. Bravo, burgundy.

During dinner there was much pleasant talk between Charles Bravo and his wife's companion. Then they all got up from table ; Mrs. Cox, as was her discreet wont, disappeared, and the husband and wife sat together for about a quarter of an hour before Mrs. Bravo went up to bed, leaving her husband in what was called the morning-room.

Charles Bravo sat on for a little while smoking. Then he himself went upstairs to his bedroom, which was next to that of his wife.

A few moments later he opened his door and shouted out, " Florence ! Florence ! Hot water ! "

Now Mrs. Bravo had already gone to sleep, and later she testified on oath that she heard nothing. But Mrs. Cox heard the cry, as did also some of the servants.

It was, however, Mrs. Cox who first hurried into Mr. Bravo's room, and it was then that he uttered to her certain memorable words on which, as we shall see, much afterwards hung.

So alarmed was Mrs. Cox by his appearance
that she went into Mrs. Bravo's room and waked
her with the news that Mr. Bravo was very ill.
Florence got up immediately, put on a dressing-
gown, and rushed to her husband's bedroom.

Charles Bravo was lying stretched out on the
floor near a window, and Mrs. Cox was rubbing
his chest.

To his wife he feebly explained that he was
"in great agony."

Already one doctor had been sent for, but,
without losing a moment, Mrs. Bravo sent off
for another, and a few minutes later she made
the groom saddle a horse and go for yet a
third, in whose medical skill her husband had
great confidence.

And then, suddenly, all three doctors arrived,
practically together, and one of them, after
seeing the patient, suggested that some noted consulting physician should be procured from town.

Florence sat down at once and wrote a note
to Sir William Gull. She sent Mrs. Cox into
London with the note, and as a result Sir
William, who was personally acquainted with
Mrs. Bravo's own family, came back in her
carriage.

Sir William Gull was not only at the head of
his honoured profession; he was a man of the
highest personal character, and it was believed
that he had saved the life of King Edward (then

Prince of Wales) by his devotion and keen intelligence.

As soon as Sir William arrived at The Priory, he and the three doctors who were already there held a short consultation. They decided that Charles Bravo's seizure was undoubtedly due to a violent irritant poison, and the three general practitioners begged their eminent colleague to try and find out what the unfortunate man had taken to account for his terrible condition.

Sir William went into Bravo's bedroom. He walked up to the bed, and, looking with pity and concern at the patient, said very gravely, "Mr. Bravo, you have taken poison."

Bravo answered feebly, "Yes; I took some laudanum."

"No," said Sir William; "you have taken something more than laudanum. And if you die without telling us, some one may be accused or suspected of having poisoned you."

Bravo replied, "I am aware of that; but I swear I have only taken laudanum, and I can tell you nothing more." He waited for a moment, and added, "I took some laudanum for my tooth."

Mrs. Bravo, though not on good terms with her mother-in-law, sent for her in the early morning, and very soon that unfortunate woman, whose only son now lay dying, arrived with her husband at The Priory.

Sir William Gull, with extraordinary kindness, for he was at the time probably the busiest professional man in London, stayed on to help the afflicted household.

Again and again he seems to have pressed Charles Bravo to try and acquaint him with the truth. But the sick man only shook his head.

At last, within a very few hours of the end, Sir William again approached the patient's bedside. Having sent everyone out of the room, he said, " I do not wish to trouble a dying man, but while you have still time, pray tell me what other poison was mixed with the laudanum." And Bravo answered, " Before God, it was only laudanum."

During those long and terrible hours, in which everyone round Bravo was doing his or her best to save his life, he showed his wife the tenderest affection. He could hardly bear her out of his sight, and yet again and again he urged her to go and lie down in order to have a little rest.

In the presence of many witnesses he further spoke to his mother of Florence's love and care of him, and he implored the older woman to be good to the younger.

His manner to Mrs. Cox was also kind and considerate.

At last, fifty hours after his seizure, and after enduring to the end a physical agony the doctors

about him found it impossible to allay, Charles
Bravo drew his last breath.

When the post-mortem examination was
made, conclusive proof was obtained that the
unfortunate man had died by the administration
of an enormous dose of antimony, a virulent
poison which is popularly known as tartar emetic.
He had swallowed no fewer than forty grains, far
more, that is, than the dose which would cause
death.   And there was a general impression
among the doctors that the poison had been
administered, or taken by him, in the burgundy
he drank at dinner.

That his stepfather suspected someone in the
house is evident, for the first thing he did—
and, of course, he had no right at all to do so in
the widow's house—was to seal up all Charles
Bravo's possessions, and to keep the keys of all
his drawers, despatch-boxes, and so on.   This
very much angered Florence Bravo, and she
wrote him a spirited letter asking him why he
had done so, and expressing surprise and indignation at his action.

IV

A sudden and unexplained death is, as we
know, always followed in England by a coroner's
inquest.   But some of us may not know that such
an inquiry may be held anywhere—in an hotel,

in a barn, even in a private house ; and immediately after Charles Bravo's death Mrs. Cox, in Mrs. Bravo's name, wrote to the coroner suggesting that the inquest should be held at The Priory, instead of, as is usual, in a public place.

She also intimated that refreshments would be provided for the jury.

This last suggestion—most improper in the circumstances, but not improper if Bravo had died from, say, a carriage or a riding accident—was complaisantly accepted by all concerned. The inquest was held at The Priory, no newspaper reporters were present, an open verdict was returned, and doubtless the jury, "twelve good men and true," enjoyed excellent refreshments at the newly made widow's expense.

But one newspaper managed, nevertheless, to obtain a report from someone who was present, and published a full account of the proceedings, which were shown to have been most perfunctory. Thus, Mrs. Cox gave evidence, but the coroner excused Mrs. Bravo, as she was ill.

This disclosure in the newspaper made it impossible for the Bravo family to regard the matter as settled.

A private consultation was held among some legal friends of Mr. Bravo.   Counsel's opinion had been taken, and it was resolved to petition the Home Secretary to order a special investigation of the case.   The jury, so far from desiring

to close the inquiry in the way which had been
done, had entered a protest against the refusal
of the authorities in the coroner's court to call
certain witnesses they urgently desired to hear.

In the result an application was made to the
Court of Queen's Bench, and Mr. William
Carter, the Surrey coroner, was directed to hold
a fresh inquest.

It was this second inquiry, held in public at the
Bedford Hotel, Balham, which, though it failed
to clear up the mystery, made it for ever famous.

The legal talent engaged strikingly showed
the importance of the case. The bereaved
mother paid a fee of a thousand pounds to the
late Sir George Lewis—then Mr. George Lewis,
junior, one of the acutest and most subtle legal
minds in England—simply to watch the proceedings. Mrs. Bravo's father, on his side,
engaged Sir Henry James, afterwards Lord
James of Hereford, an extremely sound and able
advocate, and Mr. Biron, afterwards a distinguished police magistrate, to represent her.

As the case proceeded, more counsel were
added. At first the Crown was represented by
Mr. Gorst, Q.C., afterwards Sir John Gorst,
Solicitor-General, and Mr. Poland, afterwards
Sir Harry Poland, K.C., counsel to the
Treasury and the Home Office. Later on,
the Attorney-General, Sir John Holker, ap-
peared to lead for the Crown ; and Mr. Murphy,

7*

Q.C., and Mr. Bray were briefed for Mrs. Cox.

Charles Bravo's death had undoubtedly been caused by the administration of a large dose of virulent poison, and the question now to be answered was, how he came by it ?

At first it seemed impossible to find that any motive existed which would support the theory of either murder or suicide.

Person after person testified on oath in the witness-box that Charles Bravo was happy, prosperous, ambitious, full of life and spirits. As to his private life, it soon became clear that, up to the last dread moment, his every look, his every word, breathed ardent love for his one-year wife. Many witnesses, including all their servants, declared that Mrs. Bravo, on her side, had been the kindest, the best-tempered, the most devoted of companions and helpmates to her young husband.

The only person who appeared to have the smallest motive for disliking Charles Bravo was Mrs. Cox, the quiet, discreet widow, who had for so long been Mrs. Bravo's cherished companion. It was known to a good many people that sooner or later Mr. Bravo intended to get rid of his wife's companion, but even so it was proved that they were on good terms, and that Charles Bravo always spoke kindly of her.

And then, to the amazement of the court

and of the public attending the inquiry, Mrs. Cox, finding herself in a somewhat uncomfortable position, suddenly made up her mind that "in the interests of justice" she must tell the truth as to her employer's past relations with Dr. Gully.

This disclosure was made in a sworn statement that what Charles Bravo had really said to her during that first moment of physical agony was, " Mrs. Cox, I have taken poison for Dr. Gully. Don't tell Florence !" And she went on to reveal the grim skeleton which had lurked in the dead man's House of Life.

True, Mrs. Cox modified the importance of her statement by asserting, in the most solemn way, that, " to her knowledge," the acquaintance of Florence and Gully before marriage, " though very imprudent, had been innocent in character." But whether she really intended this to be believed or not, she was soon forced to admit that in stating this she had told a deliberate lie, and that she had long been aware that the intimacy had been of a guilty nature.

At once it was seen, even by the dullest-witted, that the secret and shameful blot on Mrs. Bravo's past provided a motive, nay, more than one motive, for Charles Bravo's death—a motive for Florence Bravo, if she still perchance loved Dr. Gully ; a motive for Dr. Gully were he now a widower ; and, lastly, a motive for Bravo's suicide, if he were the type of man to destroy himself on becoming aware that his cherished wife had loved—perchance still loved—another man.

Small wonder that all England waked up to the dramatic, terrible, and pathetic under-currents of the inquiry which was now being held in the hotel at Balham.

So important had the case suddenly become that, as has been already mentioned, the Attor-ney-General appeared for the Crown, and cross-examined the principal witnesses. Serjeant Parry and Mr. A. L. Smith, afterwards Lord Justice, were briefed to watch the proceedings on behalf of Dr. Gully, and every incident of what had become Mrs. Bravo's struggle for life, as well as for honour, was waited for and followed with breathless interest.

The most important technical evidence tendered was that of the famous physician, Sir William Gull. It soon became clear that he was quite convinced of Mrs. Bravo's absolute innocence of any participation in her husband's death, and in private he again and again reiterated this belief. Sir William's statement, that in answer to one of his questions, " You are dying of poison, pray tell me how you came by it ? " Bravo replied, " I took it myself," made a great sensation ; this was, however, discounted when the great doctor had to add the words Bravo had next uttered, " I have only taken laudanum—nothing else."

Many days were spent in hearing what may be called formal evidence, that is the evidence of the other doctors who had been present during Charles Bravo's last hours, and that of the servants in the house. They, of course, were quite unable to elucidate the mystery, and it was felt that nothing " real " would be known till Mrs. Cox appeared in the witness-box. It was widely believed that this strange, quiet, apparently discreet woman held the key of the position in her hands, and when she finally stood facing the jury, and the great array of famous lawyers to whom she was about to be delivered up, it was thought that the truth must out.

But brilliant, ruthless as grand inquisitors, as were the lawyers pitted against her, Mrs. Cox proved more than a match for them all.

'Tis true that the main facts of the story— facts, we must remember, which were then quite unknown to the general public and even to the Bravo family—were dragged from her. She told, that is, the tale of poor Florence Ricardo's pitiful confession to Charles Bravo, and also of the kindly, even noble, way he had taken it. She further told how he had soon broken his promise to draw a curtain over the past, and how, instead, he had constantly taunted his wife with her secret.

Finally, Mrs. Cox solemnly reiterated her revised version of what the young man had said to her when first seized with illness, and insisted that the words were virtually a confession of suicide.

Mrs. Cox also told—and it may be imagined what a sensation the telling made—that, at Mrs. Bravo's request, she had actually gone to see Dr. Gully while Bravo lay dying. But those who had thought to find that this must surely fix the guilt on the wife were disappointed, for it soon became evident—still according to Mrs. Cox—that Mrs. Bravo's only wish had been to know what her old friend, who, it will be remembered, was also a noted physician, thought should be done to give Bravo relief in the agony he was bearing with such fortitude.

Mrs. Cox was handled very severely by the Attorney-General, whose only duty it was to ascertain where the truth lay, and whether the inquest should be followed by a murder charge. He sternly reminded the witness that she had sworn, at the first inquiry, to tell the truth, and nothing but the truth, and that she had practically confined herself to suppressing the truth in as far as in her lay.

In answer to this rebuke, the witness moved her lips, but did not reply ; " she sat as if deeply thoughtful and perplexed." She also did her best to avoid repeating aloud on the witness-stand what she had revealed as to her knowledge of the guilty relations once existing between Dr.

Gully and her friend, but the Attorney-General
forced the admission from her.

"Did you know that Dr. Gully was her
lover?" she was asked; and she finally made
the strange reply, "I think I did. I concluded
so, from his coming so often to the house."

And then she went on to make an extraordinary statement, and one which told terribly
against her unhappy friend. She suddenly observed that she was aware that at one time
Florence Ricardo had promised to marry Dr.
Gully if his wife died.

But when, after hours and hours of examination and cross-examination, Mrs. Cox stepped
down from the witness-stand, she had told
nothing that she did not mean to tell, and she
had said nothing that could really avail to
elucidate the extraordinary mystery of Charles
Bravo's death.

And then came the exciting, tense moment
for which all present at the inquiry had been
waiting—the presence of Florence Bravo, pale,
fragile, beautiful in her deep widow's weeds, in
the witness-box.

It is recorded that she was seen to be trembling violently as she kissed the Testament, and
swore the solemn oath "to tell the truth, and
nothing but the truth." But once she had done
that, she threw back the crape veil which

covered her face, and became composed, making answers to the painful and humiliating questions put to her in a firm, clear voice.

Her own counsel naturally led her to put the best complexion possible on the story. But when she came to be cross-examined by the other side, and especially by the clever lawyer who represented the Bravo family, then indeed she was faced with a terrible ordeal.

Ruthlessly was she pressed as to her past shame, and, as one of the newspapers said at the time, " It was a horrid spectacle to see a young woman, to whom reputation was evidently dear, having wrung from her, by questions as cruel as the rack, an open confession of dishonour."

Mrs. Bravo protested, in a way that was both spirited and pathetic, that her love-affair with Dr. Gully had nothing to do with her second husband's death. There came a moment, indeed, when she stood at bay and denounced her tormentors :

" That attachment to Dr. Gully has nothing to do with this case—with the death of Mr. Charles Bravo. As to that, I will answer any question. I have been subjected to sufficient pain and humiliation already, and I appeal to the coroner and to the jury, as men and as Britons, to protect me. I think it is a great shame that I should be thus questioned, and I will refuse to answer any further questions with regard to Dr. Gully."

But this moving protest was unavailing. She had to answer many more questions, and when recalling, as she was compelled to do, her husband's cruel taunts, she faltered for the first time.

Then she was made to find, and to produce, the letters Bravo had written to her, both before and since their marriage, and all sorts of matters which lawyers, as well as the general public, considered to be utterly irrelevant were elicited and added to her shame and anguish.

When counsel asked Mrs. Bravo the curious question : " Do you not feel towards Mrs. Cox the same kindly regard you always have felt ? " the witness did not answer for some time, as if analysing her feelings, and then she said, " I think she might have spared me many of these painful inquiries to which I have been subjected."

The long and ruthless examination and cross-examination of Charles Bravo's widow ended without having elicited anything that could help to elucidate the mystery of Charles Bravo's death.

But Mr. and Mrs. Bravo, senior, who, it will be remembered, had always disliked Charles's wife, had early come to the conclusion that Florence had undoubtedly done their beloved son to death, and during those first days of the inquest they spared neither trouble nor money in order to obtain the proof they sought.

At last they discovered a coachman who had been at one time in Dr. Gully's service, and later in that of Mrs. Ricardo. From him they ascertained that he had bought, on behalf of Dr. Gully, some tartar emetic seven years before.

The chemist's book was found and put in, and there was a great stir in court when the brief entry was read out :

" Name of purchaser : Gully.   Name and quantity of poison sold : Two ounces of emetic tartar."

But at once the counsel who watched the case on Dr. Gully's behalf elicited the fact that the coachman had bought the poison for treating his horses without even consulting their owner, and that the unconsumed portion of the tartar emetic had been thrown into the fire years before the marriage of Charles Bravo and Florence Ricardo !

Special value was given to this man's evidence owing to the fact that he and Mrs. Ricardo had parted on bad terms.

On the last day of taking evidence, the 22nd of the inquiry, Dr. Gully, "the aged but vigorous medico," as one of the reporters called him, leapt up on to the witness-stand. Thus these two who had once loved one another—Florence Bravo sitting in the court below, and Dr. Gully

standing in what was indeed a moral pillory—
met for the first time, if their joint evidence be
believed, since that day when they might so
truly have echoed Burns's moving lines :

> Had we never loved sae kindly,
> Had we never loved sae blindly,
> Never met or never parted,
> We had ne'er been broken-hearted!

Now it must be admitted that Dr. Gully
made an extremely good impression on the
court, on the jury, and, ultimately, on the
public.

He began by explaining that he had had no
formal notice of the inquiry, nor had he been
summoned by the coroner, but was there
entirely at his own wish. In general he confirmed Mrs. Bravo's evidence. He denied that
he had had any tartar emetic or prescribed it
in any way except in hydropathy.

One fact which came out was of very great
value to the witness—and, indirectly, to Mrs.
Bravo. It was that Mrs. Gully, though many
years older than her husband, and, therefore, at
the time of this inquiry of very great age,
was still alive and in good health. The importance of this was obvious in view of any
suspicion that Mrs. Bravo and Dr. Gully might
have been contemplating marriage on the removal of existing obstacles.

The doctor spoke with the deepest, most unaffected emotion, as he uttered the words: "On my solemn oath I declare that I had nothing whatever to do, directly or indirectly, with Mr. Charles Bravo's death. Since the marriage of Mrs. Ricardo, I have had no communication, either directly or indirectly, with that lady."

He admitted that he had seen Mrs. Cox five times, but never by his own wish—indeed, he stated plainly that at last he had given orders to his servants not to admit Mrs. Bravo's companion to his house, and that he had never withdrawn those orders.

When he came to be cross-examined by the counsel for the Bravo family, Dr. Gully had some searching questions to answer. He was asked, for instance, " You knew Mrs. Bravo had given up for you her good name and her honour, and yet you went on living close to her, which you must have known would be very painful to her husband ? "

To that Dr. Gully answered with some heat, " I did not think of Mr. Bravo in the matter. He had come between me and Mrs. Bravo, but I bore him no grudge for that. True, Mrs. Cox once said to me, ' Don't you think it would spare you pain to leave Balham ? ' But I said, ' No. I will go away for a while, but I will not give up living here.' And no suggestion

was ever made, nor was it ever suggested, that
Mr. Bravo was jealous of me. I don't know
that he ever saw me. I certainly never saw him
in my life, to my knowledge."

When Dr. Gully's ordeal was over, counsel
did not address the court as might have been
expected, but the coroner summed up. Carefully, conscientiously, he went over all the
evidence, but he was lacking—as was pointed
out at the time—in either the legal experience or
the legal acumen of a judge.

At the same time he had been specially provided with a legal assessor. Thus aided, the
coroner left, as he was bound to do, the question
who had been guilty of Charles Bravo's death
to the jury, but some thought that he made it
very plain that he himself leant, on the whole,
to the view that Charles Bravo had committed
suicide ; in any case he made it clear that in his
view there was as much evidence to show that
Bravo had done so as that he had been poisoned
by anyone else.

The jury retired to consult in private, and
during the two and a half hours of their absence
the tension became almost intolerable. Indeed,
all over the kingdom people were waiting
breathlessly for the telegram which would tell
whether the next act in the drama would be a
charge of murder brought against one or more

of the three people—the man and the two
women whom the majority of the public regarded as being either in the position of
victim or of that vilest of criminals, the secret
poisoner.

When the foreman of the jury came back, he
began by announcing that out of the sixteen
jurymen more than twelve were unanimous.

The verdict was as follows :

" We find that Mr. Charles Delauney Turner
Bravo did not commit suicide; that he did not
meet his death by misadventure ; that he was
wilfully murdered by the administration of
tartar emetic; but that there is not sufficient
evidence to fix the guilt upon any person or
persons."

As may be easily imagined, this verdict satisfied nobody, neither those closely concerned
with the conduct of the case, nor those whose
personal interest was due to their relationship to
or their affection for the dead man, nor the
thousands who had become deeply absorbed in
the tragic story.

The inquiry had lasted twenty-three full
working days; an enormous sum of money had
been spent by both the families involved, and
also by the Crown.   No fewer than forty-three
witnesses had been examined, but no conclusion
had been arrived at, and a dark cloud of sus-

picion still hung over each of those who could, by any stretch of imagination, be supposed to benefit by Charles Bravo's death.

During the second inquest the dead man's solicitor offered a reward of £500 for information showing where the antimony was obtained, and after the verdict the police offered £250 for evidence leading to the conviction of the murderer or murderers. It was all in vain.

As for Mrs. Bravo, her position preyed so much on her mind that she died within a year, and her death, surrounded by very painful circumstances, was directly attributable to the great strain and distress to which she had been subjected.

V

And now, it may be asked, what was the general consensus of intelligent opinion as to the true solution of the mystery ?

The *Times*, which had reported the case very fully and ably, devoted to it a leader of nearly a column and a half, from which we may quote the following passages :

" It is not clear upon what considerations the jury have come to the conclusion that the administration [of the dose of antimony] was not accidental but wilful, except perhaps that in case of poisoning by so rare a drug as antimony the presumption must be in favour of wilful administration.

" Although the right of examination was grossly abused, a story was elicited respecting the life of Mr. and Mrs. Bravo and of Dr. Gully which gives the two latter persons no right to complain of having been asked to explain circumstances of apparent suspicion. A more distressing picture of the consequences of indulging unlawful passion has never been drawn, and we wish we could hope that the true lesson would be deduced from it by the thousands who have devoured its unwholesome details.

" But public feeling has been revolted by the manner in which this investigation has been conducted and by the lengths to which it has been pushed. It was a cruel, and even a barbarous, act to subject a most unhappy woman to hours of cross-examination for the mere purpose of eliciting details of this connexion, and even, as in one instance, of endeavouring to extort the circumstances under which, nearly six years ago, this fatal passion arose. It was at this point that Mrs. Bravo, with a perfectly just indignation, turned on her torturers and refused to answer any more questions respecting Dr. Gully. For Dr. Gully himself no similar plea can be urged. In violation of the heavy responsibilities of his profession, and with no excuse from the passions of youth or even of middle life, he abandoned himself to a selfish intrigue, and he cannot complain of having brought himself into his present condition. But that a cross-examination even in a coroner's court of a crushed and humiliated woman should have been pushed to the length it was at Balham is a disgrace to the court which allowed it, and to the manliness of everyone who was in the least degree responsible for it."

The *Spectator* also expressed strong dissatisfaction :

" The verdict corresponds, probably, with the belief of the majority of the public, though much more evidence has been produced for the theory of suicide than was expected. Whoever is guilty or innocent, there can be no doubt that the inquiry, with all its vast expense, has broken down, and it has not during its course increased the public respect for the administration of justice. There has been, as it were, no judge ; all kinds of irrelevant matters have been introduced ; and witnesses have been allowed to contradict themselves flatly within half an hour. Indeed, as all the witnesses could read exactly what the others had said before they gave their own evidence, there was every facility for perjury, and apparently no particular desire either to prevent or to reprobate it."

Sir George Lewis, who never lost his interest in the case, formed a very definite opinion as to where the guilt lay. He scouted the notion of Charles Bravo's suicide, and to his own intimates would give his version of what he thought the truth, but professional etiquette naturally kept him silent in public.

A widely-held view, and one for which there is a great deal to be said, is that Charles Bravo, who was constantly, when in a " temper," threatening to do away with himself, may have taken laudanum on that fatal evening out of a bottle to which some person who desired to end his life had added the more violent poison of antimony.

Putting aside Mrs. Cox's evidence altogether, it is an established fact that Charles Bravo did admit, not once but several times, that he had taken poison, but it is equally clear that what he thought he had taken was laudanum, and in no very large dose. At no time, however, did he say, " I did not mean to kill myself," or " I took the laudanum by accident." On the other hand, he asserted most positively and solemnly that he had taken nothing but laudanum, when before his death all the doctors round him were aware, and plainly informed him of the fact, that he was suffering from a violent irritant poison.

There is a possible theory which has, I believe, never appeared in print before. It was formed at the time by a very able lawyer, who afterwards became a county court judge, though he was in fact equal to the highest judicial office.   This gentleman took a very strong interest in the case owing to his having had a certain acquaintance with both Mr. and Mrs. Charles Bravo.   I vividly remember his telling me that at the time of the death of Charles Bravo there was a habit among outdoor workers, especially stablemen, of playing a foolish practical joke on those of their fellows whom they · wished to annoy or tease. This consisted in putting a small quantity of antimony into their drinking water, which caused sickness but no further harm.

Charles Bravo's violent and impulsive temper must often have caused him to offend his servants, though he was always substantially just and kind in his conduct towards them.   In this connection there is a significant passage in one of Bravo's letters to his stepfather which were put in at the second inquest:

> Our third gardener is too proud for us, and cannot touch his hat or carry a parcel to the station, so I am going to give him a chance of bettering himself.   I will never keep a servant who finds that it is " not his place " to do what he is ordered to do.

My old friend's view was that one or more members of the Priory household, desiring to " pay out " the master, put some antimony in

the water-bottle in his bedroom.   It came out at
the inquest, though no importance was attached
to the fact, that Mr. Bravo, before he got into
bed, was in the habit of drinking a long draught
of water straight from the water-bottle on his
washstand.   If this is the true explanation, it is
obvious that whoever had played the practical
joke would have remained silent, and would only
have confessed if the jury had by their verdict
charged anyone with murder.

To my mind the great difficulty involved in
my old friend's theory is that Charles Bravo undoubtedly swallowed more than enough antimony
to cause death—that is to say, a much greater
quantity than any revengeful servant would be
likely to put in his water-bottle.   Indeed, in
order to account for the presence in the water-
bottle of a dose large enough to be fatal, it would
be necessary to suppose that at least two servants
had each independently on that particular evening adopted this particular method of, as they
would imagine, simply making their master
uncomfortable.   Still, it is an ingenious theory.

In the history of crime there is more than one
instance when poison has been administered and
death has been caused by the simple expedient
of adding a fatal dose to some otherwise innocuous
sleeping-draught or medicine in which a minute,
and consequently harmless, dose of the same
poison was present.

It is significant that as Charles Bravo lay dying there was none of the horror, the astonishment, the resentment which might have been expected from a healthy man suddenly struck down by poison.   That he died by an irritant poison which he did not consciously administer to himself is a fact that cannot be denied.

But who administered the antimony, and when the poison was procured, remains a mystery, and the world is as far off as it ever was from any real light on the question, " Who killed Mr. Bravo—and why ? "

APPENDIX

The following extremely interesting statement, which appeared in the *Medical Examiner* during the interval between the first and the second inquest, is given here in an appendix, partly in order to avoid interrupting the narrative and partly because it contains some medical details which all may not desire to read :

" Mr. Bravo lived at the Priory, Balham, with his wife, to whom he had been married about six months, the lady having a housekeeper, Mrs. Cox, also in the house.   On the night of Tuesday, April 18, Dr. Moore of Balham was summoned to attend Mr. Bravo.   He arrived between 9.30 and 10 o'clock, and found Mr.

Bravo lying back in a chair, breathing heavily, and totally unconscious. He was partly undressed, and Mrs. Cox was rubbing his chest. Dr. Moore, who feared the pulse would cease to beat at any minute, made inquiries of those present, but could get at nothing to account for the alarming symptoms. The heart's action was so feeble that Dr. Moore had the patient immediately placed in bed, an enema of brandy was administered, and a mustard poultice was applied over the region of the heart. Mr. Harrison, the usual family attendant, had arrived by this time, and the heart's action began to improve. Dr. George Johnson and Mr. Bravo's cousin, Mr. Royes Bell, both of King's College Hospital, having been sent for, arrived about 2.30. Just before their arrival the patient vomited for the second time. Mrs. Cox remarked that she had given him mustard, which might account for it. The first time he vomited was just before he became ill, the vomited matter being the undigested contents of his stomach, stained with Burgundy wine; the second vomit was black, and consisted of blood. He gradually improved, and at last became conscious, and complained of intense pain in the abdomen, especially in the region of the stomach. Mrs. Cox told Dr. Johnson and Mr. Bell that he had said, 'I have taken poison,' but Mr. Bravo himself, when quite conscious, denied that he had taken anything but some opium for neuralgia of the lower jaw. Dr. Johnson and Sir William Gull both pressed him on the subject, but he gave the same account of his illness. It was suggested when he was first taken ill that chloroform or opium had been taken, but the pupils were not contracted, and there was no smell of either drug. When he came to, it was clear that the symptoms were due to a powerful irritant poison. He suffered a good deal of abdominal pain, and died at 5.30 a.m. on Friday, April 21, of exhaustion.

"The post-mortem examination was made with great care by Dr. Payne of St. Thomas's Hospital, in the presence of Dr. Johnson, Dr. Moore, Mr. Bell, and Mr. Harrison. Portions of the intestines and organs were removed for careful examination and analysis. Professor Redwood had no difficulty in finding antimony, and he considered that it had been received into the body as tartar emetic. Antimony, he pointed out at the inquest, was a poison little resorted to by suicides, but it had been used by criminals to poison others, being generally used as a slow poison."

VI

THE UNWANTED CHILD

THE UNWANTED CHILD

HIPPOLYTE MENALDO

I

THE scene opens in the pretty house of the chief magistrate of one of those old-world country towns which are the glory and charm of rural France.

On a fine Sunday afternoon, while he is enjoying a little rest from his often arduous labours, a card is brought and handed to the master of the house. As he looks down at it he smiles, for it is pleasant to him to receive a call from the Marquise de Nayve, the great lady of his neighbourhood.

The Marquise and her lord inhabit a beautiful castle, originally the property of the Marquise, for she had been an heiress. They are a devoted couple, and parents of a charming daughter and of two sons, now growing up into manhood. The family enjoy what is called in France " the high consideration " of their neighbours and of their friends.

The Marquise is still a beautiful woman under forty years of age. The Marquis is a fine, distinguished-looking man, rather more intelligent, rather more bookish, perhaps, than the other country gentlemen about him. He is all the more respected owing to the fact that before his marriage, when he was poor, he held a small post in a Government office.

Eagerly the Procureur of the Republic, to give him his full style, requests that the lady be shown up. He is sorry indeed that his wife is out calling, and that, therefore, she will not have the honour of receiving a visit from the Marquise de Nayve.

But when the lady is shown into his study the shrewd lawyer at once sees that something has upset her ; and that it is the magistrate rather than the friend she has come to see and to consult. No doubt she has had some little trouble with a gamekeeper, or has been confronted with one of those difficulties which arise between landlord and tenant, even in Republican France.

After the usual rather elaborate compliments which still play so important a part in French social life, the two sit down, and the deferential host is ready to give his advice.

" You must forgive me for coming on a Sunday," she falters, " but I knew that your wife would be out to-day, and as what I want to say to you is private, I—I came this afternoon."

"I am only too pleased to see you at any time, madame. What is it I can do for you?"

"I am here," whispers at length the Marquise de Nayve, "to accuse my husband of murder, Monsieur le Procureur—of a murder committed by him nine years ago."

"You accuse your husband of murder?" repeats the magistrate, incredulously.

He feels as if he were in a nightmare; if he heard aright, then this poor lady must have gone suddenly mad. What strange delusion is this? Hastily he ransacks his brain to remember whether any of her family were insane, or suffered from delusions, but no—her father and mother were quite normal, a most commonplace old couple.

"What you tell me is very serious, madame," he murmurs.

"Yes, I know it is," she says, with a convulsive sigh. "But my conscience will no longer allow me to remain silent."

She speaks so calmly, and yet so solemnly and sadly, that the lawyer begins to fear that he is indeed about to learn some tragic secret. How tragic, how secret, he is still far from suspecting.

"And of whose murder do you accuse Monsieur de Nayve?" he asks. "I suppose you mean, madame, that your husband lost his temper and killed someone in a quarrel ? "

" No, monsieur. The murder was quite deliberate. The person whom my husband murdered nine years ago was my eldest child."

And once more the Procureur of the Republic feels as if he were living in and through a very painful nightmare. He knows that the woman who is sitting there has only had three children, who are all alive and well ; he remembers their birth, and the rejoicings thereat quite well.

But what is this the Marquise de Nayve is saying ?

" I had a child, a son, before my marriage, Monsieur le Procureur—indeed, it was because of this dark, irremediable stain on my character that my parents allowed me to marry the Marquis de Nayve. You know that, though an authentic Marquis, he was very, very poor, and that I had a fortune of sixty thousand pounds. My father, however, was an honest man, Monsieur le Procureur," and she lifts her head proudly. " The moment my parents made up their mind to allow the marriage, the Marquis was told the bitter truth."

" But you were only eighteen at the time of your wedding ! " exclaims the lawyer.

And then, for the first time, the Marquise de Nayve bursts into tears.

" Yes," she says, sobbing ; " and only sixteen

when my child was born! And I must confess that my husband has been very good to me. Never once has he reproached me. But lately he has become estranged, sombre; lately he has been anything but kind to me, and to our children he is sometimes positively brutal, and that though he loves them dearly."

"You say the Marquis killed your eldest child nine years ago? But if this child was born before your marriage, then the child at the time you say your husband murdered him was fifteen years old. How came it that he waited till then?"

"There were various reasons," says the Marquise, painfully; "reasons which I will unfold to you, Monsieur le Procureur, when I tell you the whole terrible story."

The Marquise de Nayve waits a moment, and then, in a quiet, unemotional manner, she relates what is indeed an extraordinary story, and the Procureur so far believes the amazing confession as to issue a warrant for the Marquis de Nayve's arrest on the charge of having murdered his stepson, Hippolyte Menaldo.

The warrant was executed the same evening, and though the Marquis protested his innocence with a strength that never for a moment faltered, what he admitted to be the truth was sufficiently curious and unusual to form the basis of more than one absorbing romance.

II

In every country town, and in most villages, there exist a certain number of what are called "nurse-children." Living apart from their parents, they are, in a sense, adopted by women who, in the hope of making a little money, bring them up with their own families—or, as happened in the particular case with which we are concerned, they are taken charge of by some lonely spinster, who is prepared to give her nursling all the privileges, such as they are, of an adopted child.

This was the fate, and it was, on the whole, a happy fate, which fell to the lot of the little boy who, at his birth, had been registered under the rather fantastic name of Hippolyte Menaldo.

The infant had been born at Marseilles—that is, nearly a hundred miles from the place where the parents of his unfortunate girl-mother were known and respected. When only a few days old, little Hippolyte was taken the very long journey to Orleans, and there placed in the care of a humble dressmaker named Maria Chaix.

The mother of the future Marquise de Nayve was a conscientious and a good woman. She and her husband settled two thousand pounds on their daughter's son, and it is plain that they had no wish to act unkindly or neglectfully by the poor, unwanted child. They sought out a priest, and asked if he knew a responsible person willing to take charge of a nurse-child. It was he who recommended Maria Chaix, and his choice was a very wise one. Maria was a most excellent, high-minded woman, who very soon became devotedly attached to the baby; in fact, she could not have tended him better if he had been her own child.

Time went on, and it must be admitted that those who paid Hippolyte's foster-mother the sum she received monthly for his keep by no means abandoned the little boy. Better for them, and for him, as it turned out, had they behaved as is so usual in such cases—had they, that is, offered Maria Chaix a lump sum to take charge of him for ever. Instead of doing that, his maternal grandmother kept in close touch with Maria's nursling. She came two or three times each year to see that her unknown grandchild was being properly cared for, and occasionally—not often, perhaps once every year—a young and lovely woman accompanied her.

Though Maria Chaix did not know either the name or the rank of these two ladies, she naturally came to the right conclusion—namely, that the one was the grandmother of the child of whom she had charge, and the other was the mother. It was also only too clear that the little boy Maria loved so devotedly was one of

8*

that great shadowed company of unwanted children to whom I have referred in my preface.

At last, when Hippolyte was about twelve years old, the younger lady arrived accompanied by a gentleman; they took the child out for a walk, loaded him with gifts, and behaved to him with the greatest kindness. Hippolyte's foster-mother, coming this time to the wrong conclusion, supposed the gentleman to be the child's father.

A few weeks later Maria Chaix, with inexpressible pain and, yes, resentment, received a letter telling her that the time had come when she must give up the boy in order that he might go to school. She wrote and pleaded for delay —it is even on record that she offered to keep the child henceforth for nothing, so devoted to him had she become.

But her wish was not granted, and a month later the same gentleman who had come before, and who now revealed to Maria Chaix that his name was Martin, arrived at Orleans and took the child away. He presented Maria Chaix with one hundred and fifty pounds, but in exchange he compelled her to sign a document in which she promised neither to ask for any more money, nor to try and discover the place where Hippolyte was at school.

Her evident anguish at losing the care of the little creature she had come to love so de-

votedly—to whom, indeed, she had shown herself
more than a mother—so far touched the mysterious Monsieur Martin that he informed her
that Hippolyte was about to be placed in a good
school in Savoy, where boys were educated with
a view to entering the priesthood.

Now it may here be stated that on that occasion the Marquis de Nayve—for, of course,
it was he—told the truth. He had written,
under his own name, to the Archbishop of
Savoy, asking for the address of a school where
a child could be educated with a view to his
later entering the priesthood. In answer he was
given the address of such a school or seminary,
and it was straight there that, after a heart-
breaking parting with his foster-mother, the
boy was taken by the man whom he was henceforth taught to call his guardian.

But though the school seems to have been
a fairly good school, where the boys were happy
and well cared for, little Hippolyte Menaldo,
used to the adoring love of Maria Chaix, felt
very unhappy and lonely, the more so that the
headmaster was strictly forbidden to give him
any information as to who and what he was.

The child became very studious; he showed
himself exceptionally intelligent, and at last the
Marquis de Nayve received the glad news that
young Menaldo earnestly desired to be a priest;
but in the same letter the headmaster added

that the child was terribly unhappy at being always left at school during the holidays, and he asked whether the Marquis could not arrange for the boy to go somewhere else, at any rate during the long vacations.

Now one of the curious problems of this strange story is that the Marquis de Nayve behaved far more kindly to his stepson than most men would have done in his place. He did not really neglect the child, or the child's interests; but again we may say that it would have been better for young Menaldo had he done so. He arranged for the boy to spend his summer holidays with a priest, in a pretty, cheerful country place, and during the holidays the boy received two visits from his guardian, and this time " Monsieur Martin " was accompanied by a lady who young Hippolyte was told was his godmother. She was very tender to the forlorn child, and gave him a gold watch.

As was to be expected, however, when the lad went back to school, and described to his friends his pleasant holidays and his newly-found godmother, he was soon told the truth.

" Those people," one of his older schoolfellows said to him, " are not your godfather and your godmother—they are your parents. It is too bad of them to treat you in this way, the more so that they are evidently quite rich people. Look how beautifully dressed the lady

was, and how very elegant the gentleman
always is ! "

As was only too natural, Hippolyte became
very excited and restless, and one day, while the
pupils of the school were taking a long country
walk, he ran away.   Two days later the police
found him, footsore and weary, on the road to
Orleans, and when questioned by the headmaster
as to his motive for running away, he declared
that he wished to seek out his old nurse in order
to find out who he was.

" I want to work for my living," he declared.
" I no longer wish to be a priest.   And when
I have earned a little money I shall try and find
my mother.   I am determined to know who I
am, and why such a mystery is made about it."

The head of the seminary, perplexed and
troubled, wrote and told the Marquis de Nayve
what the child had done and said, and in a few
days " Monsieur Martin " arrived at the school.
For the first time he showed himself stern, and
even angry, with Hippolyte; and after his departure young Menaldo wrote his guardian a
long and very curious letter, in which he implored him to tell him the truth.   " I have a
right to know who I am," he wrote.   " I am no
longer a child; I am fourteen."

It need hardly be said that this letter produced no satisfactory answer, and young Menaldo
soon became so restless, so idle, and so dis-

satisfied that his behaviour influenced his school-fellows in an ill sense. Soon the head of the seminary reluctantly wrote to the Marquis de Nayve, and told him that he could no longer keep his ward, the more so that it was now quite clear that Hippolyte would never make a good or happy priest. Far the best thing to do with the lad would be to put him in the way of some other means of livelihood.

As a result of this letter, the Marquis de Nayve, still, of course, masquerading as " Monsieur Martin," arrived one day at the school and took young Menaldo away. He informed the head that he was making arrangements to send Hippolyte to America, where he would be in kindly hands, and where a fine business career awaited him. Whether the Marquis ever really made such an arrangement will never be known. What is certain is that young Menaldo did not take away with him more than a change of linen, the rest of his clothes being left to be sent for when required. They never were required—and the next act in this strange, mysterious drama was to take place in Italy, and to remain secret for nine years.

III

Hippolyte Menaldo left school on a certain twenty-ninth of October, and on November the sixth some Italian fishermen found the dead body of a youth lying on the rocks which edge the sea below what is, perhaps, the most beautiful sea road in the world—that which joins Sorrento and Castellamare.

When the police were sent for, and the body had been removed to Naples, the detectives who were at once placed in charge of the case made up their minds that the corpse must be that of a French boy, for it was apparelled in the rather peculiar uniform which is only worn in French schools. On neither uniform nor underclothing was there a mark of any kind likely to lead to the identification of the dead body. Indeed, it was clear that a name had been either cut out, or picked out, of every garment clothing the bruised body. The stockings, however, were each marked with the number 56, and round the neck of the body was a medal, which showed the lad to have been a pupil at a Roman Catholic school. His age was registered as being between fourteen and seventeen.

The facts were published in all the Neapolitan papers, and several of the drivers who cater for the thousands of tourists who visit Naples each year came forward to state that on the evening of November 4 they had passed on the sea road two people who had attracted their attention.

One was a tall, good-looking man, evidently a foreigner of wealth by his general appearance and clothes, and the other was a shabbily-dressed

youth. The latter looked very weary, and
lagged so much that one of these cabmen had
actually offered to drive both walkers, for nothing, into Naples, and other drivers had pressed
their services on the walkers. But in each case
the elder man had shaken his head impatiently.

The cabmen further volunteered the fact that
about an hour after first seeing the couple they
had passed the man again, but that this time he
was alone.

The police next made inquiries at the Naples
railway station, and there one of the ticket
collectors thought that he remembered having
seen in the midnight express of November 4 a
tall, fair gentleman travelling first class, who, to
a certain extent, recalled the man described by
the cabmen.

These were the only clues, and though inquiries were made all over Italy they came to
nothing. Plenty of people wrote describing
youths and young men who had disappeared, but
it was plain that not one of them answered to the
description of the lad who had been dashed to
death on the rocks below Castellamare. At last
all efforts to discover the identity of the unfortunate young stranger, who had met his death in
so horrible a way, were dropped. The body was
buried, and the affair was classed among those
unsolved mysteries with which the police are
more often confronted than is generally supposed.

To return to the Marquis de Nayve. His wife always declared that when he left home on October 28 she never knew where he had gone, or on what business. Be that as it may, the Marquise was able to produce a letter written from Marseilles on November 9, in which her husband told her, with the greatest detail, of a very unfortunate adventure which had befallen Hippolyte Menaldo and himself.

According to this letter, the Marquis had taken the lad straight from Savoy to Italy in order to give young Menaldo a pleasant holiday before sending him to America. They had gone from Rome to Florence, and thence to Naples. It was there, while they were taking a walk on the famous sea-wall road, that suddenly, in the darkness—the Marquis admitted that this strange walk had taken place at night—the boy had escaped from him and disappeared !

The Marquis added that he had not been as surprised as he might have been, for Hippolyte violently objected to the American plan, and had threatened to run away. In the letter in which he told his wife this story was enclosed, without comment, a cutting from a Marseilles paper in which was told the pitiful tale of the finding of the body of a nameless youth who had met his death on the rocks below Castellamare.

The Marquis himself followed this strange letter home a day or two later, and then he did a very curious thing—a thing which certainly stood him in good stead during the trial which was to take place nine years later.

A man guilty of murder, so naturally argued those who believed in the Marquis's innocence—and there were many such all over France—would have gone back to his château and kept secret for ever, save perhaps from his unhappy wife, his version of the tragic happening at Castellamare.

This, however, was not the course pursued by the Marquis de Nayve. Hardly had he been home a week before he asked two distinguished lawyers who were among his friends, and also his parish priest, to come and see him. To them all three he told the story contained in the letter written at Marseilles. Then he solemnly asked their advice as to whether it was his duty to communicate with the Italian police.

After conferring together for a considerable time, they advised him to remain silent. Nothing could now bring Hippolyte Menaldo to life again, and if the Italian police were once put on the track of the dead boy's identity, the long-kept secret of the Marquise, now an honoured wife and the mother of three children, would inevitably be revealed.

But the Marquis de Nayve's troubles were by no means over. Even in the provincial French papers the story of the discovery near Naples was being published as an exciting piece of news, much being made of the fact that the Italian police believed the corpse to be that of a child of French extraction, or one who had been to a French school. The fact that the number 56 was on his stockings was also stated.

Thereupon the Marquis rushed off to the Savoy seminary. Once more he told his version of the terrible story—this time to the head-master; the latter evidently believed him, for not only did he keep the secret for nine long years, but he transferred the number which had been young Menaldo's to another boy.

The Marquis de Nayve breathed again; but he had reckoned without Maria Chaix. The boy had written to her, paying one of the school servants out of his scanty pocket-money to post his letters; and when these ceased coming the poor woman became exceedingly unhappy and anxious. After a while she actually wrote to two or three people in the neighbourhood of the seminary asking if anything had happened to young Menaldo, and one of her correspondents went to the trouble of finding out that the child was no longer at the school. Maria Chaix then wrote a most pathetic letter to the headmaster, imploring him to tell her what had happened to her nursling, and asking to be given his new address.

On being informed of this letter the Marquis

went off to Orleans, but when there he did not seek out Maria Chaix herself ; instead he went to see the priest who had recommended the woman fifteen years before. He told the priest that the poor nurse-child had been drowned while taking a walk near his school, and he also said that, in view of the fact that he was no longer paying for the boy's education, and because Maria Chaix had been so extremely kind to Hippolyte, he meant to allow her henceforth a pound a week.

But Maria Chaix refused to believe the boy was dead. She went on trying to discover where he was, and finally her friend the priest received a letter from the Marquis de Nayve informing him that if Maria persisted in these inquiries her pension would be stopped.

This threat served its purpose, and for something like seven years the Marquis lived a peaceful life, honoured by all who knew him, and passionately devoted to his children, although sometimes showing himself strangely brutal in his treatment of them.

IV

The trial of the Marquis de Nayve for the murder of his stepson took place at Bourges, in the splendid mediæval palace where once lived that French hero of romance, Jacques Cœur.

In addition to the prisoner at the bar, there

were present in court the Marquise and her two sons, aged sixteen and eighteen ; also, one need hardly add, all the more notable people of the neighbourhood.

The prisoner was defended by Maître Danet, one of the foremost leaders of the French Bar. It was unfortunate for the prosecution that Maria Chaix had died while the Marquis was awaiting his trial. But she was represented by a friend, a Madame Garnier, who was allowed to give a great deal of what we in England would call most irrelevant evidence.

Madame Garnier had brought with her to the court what neither the Marquis nor the Marquise knew she possessed—a whole bundle of letters from the doomed child, written to his devoted foster-mother

The French are an emotional people, and there were few dry eyes in court while the pathetic letters of the little boy were being read out.

My darling Nurse,
How can I ever thank you enough for all you have done for me. When I was cold you warmed me ; when I was hungry you fed me. You always took the greatest care of me, and when I am a big man I will come and live with you, and be the staff of your old age. Every day when I say my prayers I ask God to give you a long and

happy life. We may never meet again
dear Maria, but God will protect you, and
one day we shall find each other out in
heaven.

Then came other letters, as the child grew
older,—letters in which he showed only too
clearly how bitterly he felt his peculiar position.

Oh, Maria, I am so unhappy! All the
other boys here have a father and a mother,
or at least a mother. Sometimes I feel as
if I should burst with grief. I love you,
Maria, with all my heart. No one will ever
make me give you up. As for that Monsieur
Martin, he is so unkind, he will not tell me
how you are. Oh, if only I were grown up
—if only I were twenty-one! Do not fear
I shall ever forget you who loved me, who
brought me up, who nourished me. You
are my mother, Maria, my adopted mother.
The days do drag, Maria, though no one
here is exactly unkind to me. I kiss you
very tenderly. I do not forget you. But
what I want you to tell me, Maria, is the
name of my mother. You don't know how
worried I feel. The other boys all have a
mother. Their mothers write to them, they
write to their mothers. I feel as if I can't
go on working. I wish you would come
and see me.

And then Madame Garnier, who had known
little Hippolyte from his birth, told of Maria's

efforts to find what had become of the child, and
of the threat, transmitted to Maria by the
priest, that her pension would be stopped if she
went on with her search.

When the good woman's evidence was ended,
there came forward certain Italians, inn-keepers
and others, who told the story of the Marquis
de Nayve's strange, hurried flight—for flight it
seemed—through Italy. He had taken the child
there, or so he said, for a pleasant little holiday,
yet the two had spent hardly any time at all in
sight-seeing. From Milan they had rushed to
Genoa, thence to Rome, on to Florence, finally
to Naples—and always travelling by night.

An interesting witness was an Italian gentleman, who came forward to explain that he had
shared a first-class compartment with the ill-
assorted couple on their journey to Naples.

He particularly remembered the fact that
the elder of his fellow-travellers had made the
boy with him change his stockings. That had
struck him so much that he had put down the
fact in his diary—and this diary was put in at
the trial. It proved, however, nothing else, save,
perhaps, that the Marquis had overlooked the
fact that the number 56 was on the stockings,
while aware that there was no name on them.

It was also shown that on the night of
Hippolyte's disappearance the unfortunate boy
and his stepfather had walked about Naples for

hours ; in fact, the distance they had gone on foot had been something like twelve to fifteen miles. Thus, when they reached the spot where the boy was supposed to have run away, he must have been quite worn out, and so tired as hardly to know what he was doing.

And then came that terrible questioning and cross-questioning of the accused, an ordeal which was formerly unknown in British law, though it may now take place, strictly safeguarded, if the prisoner elects to go into the witness-box.

" Why, if the boy ran away from you, did you not raise an alarm—send notice to the police ? "

" You ask me that, sir ?   How little you understand what was then my position !   Had I done so, I should have had to reveal who the child was—I should have had to compromise my wife's honour, to betray her secret."

" Nonsense !   There is no shame in having an illegitimate child."

Said the Marquis coldly, " That may be your view, sir ; it is not mine."

And it must be admitted that the audience thought the prisoner, not his cross-examiner, in the right.

The headmaster of the school where young Menaldo had been was called, and severely censured for having kept the Marquis de Nayve's secret ; so also were the two lawyers and the priest.

The prosecution set forth a terrible indict-
ment ; but it was clear that the Public Prosecutor
did not expect a verdict. The time gone by
had been so long, the precise manner in which
the child had met his death was still wrapped in
so great a mystery !

When the Marquise went into the box, she
had to admit that she had no proof—only that
she suspected her husband of having done away
with the child ; never, never had he altered or
modified his first, and only, story.

And then, when the prisoner's two sons were
put into the box, public opinion veered round in
favour of the Marquis. The boys spoke warmly,
affectionately, of their father ; true, he had
been severe, but not more severe than they
deserved.

Half a dozen well-known and highly-respected
local magnates came forward and generously
swore on oath that they had always had a high,
a very high, opinion of the Marquis de Nayve,
and that they still thought him incapable of
committing a dastardly crime. He was a man
of honour, a man against whom no one had ever
been heard to say anything with regard to his
private character or to his money dealings with
his fellow-men.

Maître Danet, in his speech for the defence,
drew an eloquent picture of the anguish this
honourable, high-minded gentleman had felt in

the knowledge that there existed in the world a human being whose mere existence was fraught with bitter shame to his wife.

" And yet, take notice, gentlemen," he continued, addressing the jury, " of this fact, that neither the Marquis nor the Marquise did what so many people do in such a case—they made no efforts at any time to get rid of the child, and of their duty to him, once for all, by payment of one lump sum. On the contrary, they took the greatest trouble to see that he was put in a respectable and good school. More than that, they paid him, I will not say frequent, but occasional visits, and told him to regard them as his godfather and godmother—a relationship to which much more importance is attached in this country than elsewhere. Finally, they pensioned handsomely the woman who had looked after him."

And then the defence were able to put into the box certain of young Menaldo's schoolfellows, now grown-up men, who solemnly swore that they had heard him, not once but many times, threaten to commit suicide.

" As to why the Marquis kept silent after that tragic journey in Italy, you have only to ask yourselves, gentlemen, what you would have done in his place," cried the famous lawyer. " Would any one of you have acted differently ? Would any one of you, knowing that this poor unwanted child was dead, that nothing could bring him to life again, have gone and dishonoured your wife, the woman you cherished, and who was the mother of a daughter and of sons whom you loved, by revealing her pitiful and shameful secret? I confidently say No, you would not have done so—you would have acted exactly as did my client!"

Up to the last moment it seemed uncertain what the verdict would be. The jury stayed away for some hours, but at last they came back into the court, and, amid a dead silence, gave their verdict of "Not guilty."

The Marquis de Nayve was free!

The two boys rushed to their father and clasped him, as is the emotional French fashion, in their arms; and within a week it was known that he and his wife had become reconciled.

VII

A WOMAN'S HONOUR

A WOMAN'S HONOUR

THE CHAMBIGE AFFAIR

THERE is nothing rarer than an undiscovered human mystery. The few real mysteries there are in history may be counted on the fingers of one hand. Was Mary Queen of Scots the writer of the Casket Letters? Who was the Man in the Iron Mask? Were the shameful allegations brought by Mrs. Beecher Stowe against Byron true? Thousands and thousands have asked themselves these questions, and a whole literature has grown and is still growing round each of them.

In the Chambige affair, the curious student of human nature, and the investigator in crime, is confronted with a mystery which lies deep in the roots of humanity, those roots from which spring the upas trees of passion, hate, jealousy, and fear. It was, as we shall see, the mysterious element in the story which made it, at the time it happened, arouse such fierce feelings of partisanship that all over France there were households where the subject had to banned, the women, with scarce an exception, taking part of their fellow-woman, the men the part of their fellow-man.

The object of the account which follows is show how curiously the facts seem to support each of the two possible explanations in turn, and to leave the reader to form his own judgment as to where the truth lies.

I

On one of those beautiful and pleasantly hot afternoons which often visit the north of Africa in the winter, a young Frenchman named Henri Chambige hailed a cab on the great square of the town of Constantine.

The driver knew quite well who his fare was. This ugly, excitable-looking youth belonged to the ruling class of the colony of Algiers. He was generous and kind-hearted, and, what to French people in any class of life would seem of more consequence, Henri Chambige, in spite of his being only three-and-twenty years of age, was already a distinguished literary man.

Young Chambige told the cabman he wished to be driven out to Sadi Mabrouk, a suburb of the town. Then he gave the address of a certain Madame Grille.

The driver also knew all about the Grilles. Monsieur Jacques Grille was the chief engineer of the Algerian railway system; his wife, Madeleine, was rather younger than her husband, and in spite of the fact that her hair had turned prematurely white, she was still considered a very pretty woman. Madame Grille was exceptionally kind-hearted and sweet-natured, a tender mother to her two little daughters, and a most devoted wife to her husband. Of English origin,—her maiden name was Jackson,—her marriage to the French engineer had been the outcome of a charming romance, for he had been poor, she rich, and they had waited for each other almost as long as Jacob waited for Rachel.

The fact that the cab-driver knew Madame Grille is worth mentioning, for his subsequent evidence proved that, even among a class ready to suspect evil, Madeleine Grille was regarded as above suspicion.

To return to the fateful day on which the mysterious tragedy took place which was to make the world ring with this poor lady's name.

When he had arrived at his friends' villa, Henri Chambige went into the house, and after a few minutes came out again, accompanied by Madame Grille and a woman servant, to whom she remarked :

9

" I am just going with Monsieur Chambige to
his mother's villa. Please see that the children
have their tea when they have done playing in
the garden."

The villa to which Madame Grille referred
was in the country, two miles from her house,
and some time before she had kindly offered the
owner, young Chambige's mother, to keep the
keys and see that the house was occasionally
aired and opened.

On the way to the villa Henri Chambige
behaved in rather an odd way, so the cab-driver
thought. He began singing, at the top of his
voice, a song then popular in France, the first
line of which ran " Good-bye, last morning of
my life ! "

When at last they reached the empty villa,
Henri Chambige helped Madame Grille to
alight from the open carriage. " You will have
to wait a little while," he said to the driver, " for
we shall probably stay here some time."

The two went up the steps of the villa—Henri
Chambige, the lad of three-and-twenty, and
Madeleine Grille, the charming, delightful
woman of three- or four-and-thirty—and disappeared through the front door. Then Chambige, turning, did a rather singular thing—he
locked the house door behind himself and his
companion.

There followed what seemed to the cabman

outside an interminably long wait, in the hot, still air, and as the minutes dragged on the driver wondered more and more why these people were making such a long stay in the house.

At last, after two hours had gone by, there came the sound of a pistol shot.

Then, once more, dead silence.

Jumping hurriedly down from the carriage, the cabman tried to make his way into the villa, but the lock of the front door stood fast. Again he got up on to his seat, and again there came the sharp, thudding sound of two shots; and a moment later two young men, friends of Chambige, hurried up to the door. They had come, in apparently breathless haste, and on foot, from the town of Constantine.

" Is Monsieur Chambige here ? " they asked anxiously.

" Yes," said the driver. " He has been in the villa ever so long with Madame Grille, and a few moments ago I heard shots being fired."

" We fear something terrible has happened ! " they both exclaimed. " Will you help us to break our way into the villa ? "

By breaking a window at the back, the three men succeeded in entering the house, and then, hearing no sound, they wandered through the sunny lower rooms.

Finding nothing, they went up the staircase

leading to the upper floor, and there, in the principal bedroom, a terrible sight met their eyes.

Lying dead on a couch near the bed was Madame Grille. Writhing in agony on the floor by her side was Henri Chambige, with blood streaming from two bullet-holes through his cheeks.

As the men came in, he was stretching out his hands for the revolver with which his wounds, and the wound that had killed Madeleine Grille, had evidently been inflicted.

" Let me die ! " he cried wildly. " I refuse to outlive her ! Let me die ! "

One of his two friends snatched the revolver from his hand ; and then the three men began to make desperate, futile efforts to bring the dead woman to life again. But she had been shot in the temple ; death must have been practically instantaneous.

With bewildered horror and pain, at last they left the body of the unfortunate woman alone in the villa, and transported their friend, whose wounds they thought were far more serious than they turned out to be, back to his stepfather's house in Constantine, leaving word, on the way, at the Villa Grille of the awful thing that had happened.

II

Judicial procedure in France is very different from that which obtains in any English-speaking country.

In France, as most of us know, the first thought of the examining magistrate is to get at the truth without any particular consideration for the feelings of the possible criminal. Accordingly, within an hour of young Chambige's return to Constantine, he was being pressed with eager questions by the official concerned— who, by the way, was an intimate friend of Monsieur and Madame Grille.

At first Henri Chambige refused to say anything; indeed, he did nothing but repeat, in varying tones of anguish, despair, revolt, and longing: "Let me die! I only wish to die! Why did I not kill myself? How is it that I have outlived *her*?"

At last, however, amid sighs, groans, and tears, and speaking with great difficulty—for the wounds in his cheeks, though not dangerous, were exceedingly painful—young Chambige told the magistrate an extraordinary, and to his listener an incredible, story.

"I loved Madeleine Grille!" he exclaimed dramatically, "and she loved me! Rather than lead a life of deceit, rather than embark on an illicit love - affair, we decided to die to-gether——"

Now, the magistrate was not only Monsieur Grille's intimate friend; he also had a great regard and respect for his friend's wife. It seemed to him inconceivable that the woman he had known for years as a loving wife, and as a devoted, over-anxious mother, could have cherished a secret passion for this youth, who was not only twelve years younger than herself, but, from any other man's point of view, most unattractive.

" Impossible ! " cried the magistrate indignantly. " Chambige, I am sure that you are lying ! Remember that you will have to prove this incredible assertion of yours before any credence will be given to your word."

But, though the worthy magistrate did not believe Chambige's story, the facts themselves spoke with a terribly silent eloquence.

Why had Madame Grille accompanied the young man to the empty house ? How was it that there was no sign of a struggle having taken place ? It looked as if the dead woman had composed herself for sleep before the fatal shot was fired.

We have all experienced the state of mind that makes us say, " I should not believe it, even if I were to see it with my own eyes ! "

Such was the noble attitude of poor Madeleine

Grille's husband. From the first horrible moment when he learned the awful facts of the case, he behaved with dignity and restraint. He refused even to consider the question of his wife's dishonour; he denied with cold scorn the possibility of her having had an infatuation for Henri Chambige. And his attitude was shared by Madeleine's many friends and relations.

But Henri Chambige was not without many devoted allies, who all declared him to be incapable of telling a lie. Friends of his travelled all the way from Paris to testify on oath that for the last two years they had been aware that he had a serious, absorbing love-affair in his life, which had transformed him from a rather fast, reckless young man to a sober, thoughtful worker.

The only proof he was able to adduce of the truth of his strange story were certain entries in his own diary. For Henri Chambige, like many young Frenchmen of his type, kept a very elaborate diary, in which he put down, not only what happened day by day, but the varying state of his mind, heart, and conscience. Though he was thus able to prove how absorbing and how morbid had been his passion for the woman who, *whatever the truth*, was certainly in one sense his victim, he was unable to show a single scrap of Madame Grille's handwriting.

At the request of the legal authorities, he wrote,

during the time which elapsed between the tragedy and his trial for murder, a long account of the secret passion which he asserted had united Madeleine Grille and himself.

That statement and the diary were his only defence. Could he prove his story true—could he, that is, persuade judge and jury that Madame Grille had arranged to die with him by her own wish, his acquittal was certain, and he would join the long roll of Frenchmen who have thought the world well lost for love.

III

Henri Chambige was the only son of a well-known lawyer of Algiers. But his youth was shadowed by the fact that his father committed suicide. He had, however, a fond mother, and, though she married again, the tie between herself and her son was in no sense weakened, and a large sum was spent on his education.

He soon showed that he possessed marked literary gifts. At the age of eighteen he published a volume of verse which was favourably received, and two years later he began a curious philosophical work on the effects of the passion of love on the brain.

In spite of his plainness of appearance and his delicacy of health, there was something very attractive about Henri Chambige, and he soon became a well-liked member of Paris literary society.

On his twenty-first birthday his mother begged him to come and spend a long holiday with her at Constantine, where she lived with her second husband and with her young married daughter. He did so, and it was then that there took place his first meeting with the woman who, according to his own account, was to exercise so strange and so disastrous an effect on his life.

Madeleine Grille and the sister of Chambige were intimate friends, and Madame Grille frequently came to the house where the young man was spending the winter ; but in those early days they seem simply to have formed a pleasant acquaintanceship. The young poet sometimes called on the Grilles, and was kindly welcomed by both husband and wife. And then, in due course, he went back to Paris.

Months went by, and in the following July the married sister, to whom the young man had been greatly devoted, suddenly died.

Chambige hastened to Constantine in order to comfort his mother, and his friendship with his dead sister's intimate friend became closer, the more so that the Grilles were themselves in the saddest mourning, for they, in the interval, had lost their only son, a child of three.

I saw Her again through a veil of tears [noted Chambige in his strange *apologia*].

9*

The day after my arrival in Constantine she came to the house. I saw Her alone. It was as if I saw Her for the first time. I opened my heart and entreated Her to enter its inmost secret chamber. I revealed to Her my most intimate thoughts. She listened, full of silent, intense sympathy. And then she also began telling me of her terrible loss and grief. She also allowed me to enter her heart. Oh, God! Oh, God! What would I not do to see you again, my Beloved?

And after that day—that day of revelation—we were never happy unless we were together. Sad and mournful were we when Fate drove us apart! Every evening I used to ride from my mother's villa to Her house, bringing her a bunch of flowers. . . . But I never told my love; and then, one day, she saw that I was indeed unhappy. With an impulsive gesture, Madeleine, my pure angel, put her hand on my shoulder in order to console me. Her touch filled me with burning joy and anguish. " Pity me ! " I cried. " Yes, you may indeed pity me ! " And then, suddenly, she told me that she loved me, and that she had loved me from our first meeting. . . . As for me, I fell on my knees, as I would have knelt before a saint from Paradise.

But Madeleine thought our love was wicked. It was agony to Her to feel that she was being, even in this comparatively innocent sense, unfaithful to Her husband.

" I feel as if I must tell him the truth,"
she sometimes cried. But I implored Her
not to do so. After all, we were doing
nothing wrong, and I told Her that if she
confessed the truth to her husband he
would almost certainly suspect that there
had been far more in our friendship than
there had been. She then implored me to
leave Constantine. I did so . . .

And whether Chambige was telling the truth
or, as Madeleine Grille's friends believed, roman-
cing—there is no doubt that he did leave
the colony abruptly, in spite of his mother's
wish that he should stay on through the
winter.

Further, several of his intimates testified that
on his return to Paris the poet confided, first to
one and then to another, that he was in love
with a married woman in Algiers, and that his
passion was so absorbing that he could neither
think nor work. He did not, however, reveal
her name, or confide to even his closest friends
any of the circumstances of the case.

Time went on, and in January Henri Chambige
received a telegram informing him of the sudden
serious illness of his mother. He set off instantly,
and arrived at Constantine to find her a little
better. It was then, according to that strange,
pathetic statement which formed his only " defence," that the pent-up passion surging in his

heart and in that of Madeleine Grille suddenly
burst forth.

They felt that they could not again part—
and part platonic friends.

But there came a day when the young man
felt he must return to Paris. On the morning of
the day he intended to leave for France, he rode
out to Madame Grille's house to say farewell,
for he was aware that her husband was absent
on business. They met, or so he said—her
servants vehemently denied it—secretly, in the
lovely garden of the villa.

> " I cannot let you go again ! " she cried,
> bursting into tears. " Ah, if only I were
> young, we might begin life together——"
> I fell at Her knees, intoxicated with joy
> and pride. " Yes," I cried, " let us go
> away ! Only give me a few hours in
> which to find some money, and we will
> flee together."

And there was plenty of proof that young
Chambige spent the rest of that morning and
part of the early afternoon trying to procure
a loan of five thousand francs. He was accompanied, during the whole of his fruitless quest,
by a young man, who was one of the two
who followed him to the deserted villa.

This friend had to leave Chambige for half an
hour on business of his own, and it was during

that half-hour that the poet bought a revolver and some ammunition.

At last he drove, as we know, back to the Villa Grille. He rushed into the house—we are following his own account—and told the woman he loved that, as he had not been able to find the money, he was going away, back to Paris, alone.

> Perhaps my wild manner or some word or two I let drop filled Madeleine with a terrible—a true suspicion.
>
> "I know what you are going to do," she cried. "You are going to kill yourself! Rather than that, let us die together!"
>
> Hurriedly she put on her hat and lace cloak, and it was at her suggestion that I told the driver of my cab to take us to my mother's villa.
>
> During our last drive together she bade me sing, and as I sang she whispered to me what she had determined we should do. "You must kill me first," she murmured, "for you, being a man, have more courage than I. I ask you to promise me, by all you hold sacred, that you will kill me first."
>
> And I gave her my promise!
>
> We went into my mother's room, and there we sat down and had a long, ecstatic talk. I recited to her the verses I had written to her when we were far apart, and I reminded her of the many lovers who, since the world began, had died together.

I also told her that all who had ever loved purely, passionately, as we did, would understand and defend us.

" The only thing that makes me miserable," she said, " is the awful thought of the way in which my death will dishonour my children."

" No, no ; the whole world will admire us," I cried. . . .

Before preparing to die she said to me, very gently :

" I feel at once exquisitely content and exceedingly miserable. But I love thee —I love thee !" She herself arranged the muzzle of the revolver against her temple, and gave me the signal to pull the trigger. Then I turned the revolver against my own temple, but the Fates were cruel, and compelled me to live.

So ended the sworn statement of Henri Chambige.

IV

And now comes the terrible mark of interrogation to which such varying answers were given. Did Henri Chambige *invent* the whole of this strange, sad story, from a morbid wish to become infamously famous ?

Is it possible that Madeleine Grille, to all appearance an exceptionally happy wife, and certainly a most devoted mother, fell violently in love with a man of whom she had seen comparatively little, and who was so much younger than herself? Further, is it credible that, discovering the young man's intention of destroying himself, such a woman as was Madeleine Grille would have insisted on their dying together?

"No; neither the one nor the other is possible or credible!" So declared with one voice a formidable cloud of witnesses—including her loving, faithful husband, her mourning mother, her brothers and sisters, and her host of friends. They were unanimous in saying that Madeleine Grille was kind to this young man, this hysterical, morbid poet, simply because he was the brother of her dead friend. Chambige was sad, delicate in health, and dreadfully sensitive. She allowed him to come constantly to her house because he was idle and she was good-natured. Nay, more; she had even confided to certain of her friends that she found these constant visits of young Chambige a considerable worry in her busy, well-filled life.

And not only the friends and relations of Madame Grille, but all those in the colony who belonged to her own Huguenot faith, including her respected pastor, took the same view of her character and behaviour.

They pointed out that she was no actress, and that she could not have played the part that he attributed to her; also, whether she was or was

not in love with Chambige, there could be no
doubt that, during the months their attachment
was said by him to have been at its height, she
was behaving to her husband as does a fond
and most devoted wife.

Besides this, she was in daily communication
with her mother, to whom she was telling all the
little details of her daily life, including her constant care of her little girls' health and happiness.
True, she had felt terribly the death of her young
son. But she was beginning to recover from
her grief; and in one of her letters she had
hinted that she hoped some day to have another
child.

V

We come now to the trial of Henri Chambige
for the murder of Madeleine Grille.

Seldom had a case produced more angry and
vehement discussion. The court was filled with
enemies, for every person present either regarded
the prisoner in the dock as a hero, or as a
dastardly murderer, who, not content with killing his victim, had tried also to destroy her
honour.

After the medical evidence had been heard at
great length, the Public Prosecutor put Monsieur
Grille into the box. Dressed in deep mourning
but showing only restrained emotion, and carefully averting his eyes from the bowed figure in

the dock, the husband of Madeleine gave his evidence in measured tones.

" I can only affirm," he declared, " by all I hold most sacred, and before the God in whom I believe, that I am as sure as I am of my own life that my wife was faithful to me in thought, word, and deed during the whole of our married life. We fell in love when we were very young —she was only sixteen. She waited for me, although she had many offers, for six years—till I was well enough off to make a home for her. No woman was ever a kinder, a better, and a sweeter wife than she was to me, and that to the very day of her——" He waited a moment, and then deliberately uttered the word " murder."

" I do not wish to go into the matter of that man's shameful assertions," he continued. " Chambige is a madman. I pity him as I do every lunatic who is afflicted with homicidal mania. I cannot tell you why he has brought this disgraceful accusation against my poor wife, but I am sure that he is not able to help it. He speaks thus because he is distraught."

This evidence of Monsieur Grille naturally made a very deep impression on the jury—it was plain that he believed every word that he said.

Then the mother of the dead woman came and stood in the witness-box. Speaking in trembling accents, and with far more feeling than the hus-

band had chosen to show, she assured the jury
that her daughter had been the happiest of wives,
the most tender and careful of mothers, without
a thought beyond her home and the interests of
her husband and her children. She read to the
jury the happy, cheerful letter which had been
broken off in the middle of a sentence in order
that Madame Grille might accompany young
Chambige to the fatal villa.

" You may wonder, gentlemen," said the poor
woman, " why my daughter went off, like that,
to his mother's empty villa with Henri Chambige.
And yet the explanation is very simple. She
had promised to look after the villa during the
lady's illness, and, as young Chambige was
leaving the colony that day, there were certain
things of his which he wanted to fetch away.
She was willing to go with him and to have the
pleasant drive, for it was a very hot day. As to
why this man killed my daughter, I can only
agree with my son-in-law ; from my point of
view, Chambige is a degenerate and a maniac."

And then there followed a long string of
witnesses, including the servants of the dead
woman. They testified that they had never
seen anything in the least peculiar in her manner
to the young man, and they also swore on oath
that they had heard her more than once speak
with annoyance of his constant visits. Indeed,
she had actually given orders at one time that

if he came in the morning, when she was busy with her accounts and household matters, he was not to be admitted!

Then the defence called Henri Chambige's relations and friends to testify to their high opinion of the poet's honour and truthfulness. Those of his friends who were able to swear that he had spoken to them of his love for a married woman in Algiers were listened to very coldly, both by the jury and the public; for, whatever may happen in practice, in theory no man ever talks of such an affair, even to his closest and dearest friend.

This unwritten law of honour young Chambige had, to a certain extent, broken; not to one, but to many, had he spoken of his love, his adoration, of a married woman in the far-off colony where his mother dwelt. But he had never told anyone her name.

There followed eloquent speeches from both the prosecution and the defence. Henri Chambige's family naturally engaged a great advocate, Maître Durien, to defend him, and it may easily be imagined how such a case would be treated by a Frenchman, and how strong would be his appeal to the romantic sensibilities of the jury.

As for the Public Prosecutor, Maître Trarieux, he violently attacked poetry and romance, holding that the Muses were largely responsible for the tragedy. As there were no poets or romancers on the jury, his remarks produced a greater impression than they would otherwise have done.

The judge summed up "dead" against the prisoner, and Henri Chambige was solemnly condemned to death. The sentence was, however, commuted, within a very few days of the end of the trial, by the President of the Republic.

We cannot doubt that to the end of time the *affaire Chambige* will remain one of the greatest judicial mysteries ever tried.

On the one side stands the young man's own connected and consistent account of a great passion which death alone could keep pure and untarnished. On the other stands the unanimous testimony of all who knew the hapless object of this passion—that she was incapable of a disloyal thought, and that, even supposing she had been stricken with so unlikely an infatuation, she could not have concealed it for a day from those around her, so frank, sincere, and unaccustomed to deceit was her whole nature.

It is an interesting fact that for a brief time Chambige was what is called a "holiday tutor" in the household of "Gyp," the famous novelist. She formed a very poor opinion of the young man's mental state, and, shortly after the tragic events here related, she wrote a novel, called *Un Raté*, in which she retold the story in her own way.

VIII

WHERE PLATONIC LOVE MAY LEAD A MAN

WHERE PLATONIC LOVE
MAY LEAD A MAN

THE PELTZER AFFAIR

I

ONE fine cold January morning the prosperous Antwerp barrister, William Bernays, kissed his little boy, said good-bye to his wife—he was not on kissing terms with his wife—and took train for Brussels.

Neither wife nor child ever saw him again.

William Bernays had said he meant to come back that same night, but no word was received from him to account for his absence. After two anxious days of waiting and of wondering what could have happened to prevent her husband's communicating with home, Madame Bernays informed the police of his disappearance.

Oddly enough, no one at first knew what business had taken the lawyer to Brussels ; but soon that trifling mystery was cleared up. An acquaintance whom he had met in the train, and who had travelled with him a short distance, remembered that Bernays had casually mentioned the fact that he was about to meet an important new client. " The man appears to be an American, in a big way of business," Bernays had observed. " I've not seen him yet, but we've been in correspondence, and he's already sent me a hundred and fifty dollars."

No trace of this unknown American client's letters, or of the cheque he had sent, could be found among the lawyer's papers, and the disappearance of William Bernays became a nine days' wonder in the town of Antwerp.

In such a case the very last thing that people are apt to suspect is what is popularly called foul play, and William Bernays' old friends and lifelong neighbours had more than one theory which might account for his temporary disappearance.

Not long before his mysterious journey to Brussels, the lawyer had become a Roman Catholic, and certain people thought it conceivable that he had gone off to a monastery.

Others recalled, under their breath—for his beautiful young wife was respected and even beloved—that William Bernays, like so many clever, brilliant men, had an ugly side to his nature—a very different one, that is, from his religious side. He had never been a man of high moral character. Madame Bernays was a saint, and from a sinner's point of view a saint is sometimes "gey ill to live with," as many an average man has discovered to his cost.

Was it not possible that Bernays had gone on a short illicit honeymoon? If popular rumour spoke truly, this would not have been the first time. And Madame Bernays, noble woman that she was, had forgiven and forgotten. Many a man in Antwerp envied the lawyer his happy, successful, careless life, and his fair if austere wife.

But just a few members of his own family, and one or two trusted friends and confidants outside that narrow circle, knew that William Bernays was not the happy man he appeared to be.

True, he seemed to possess everything that makes for happiness in this world. He had a great reputation in his profession, he was blessed with plenty of money, he had a delightful home, and a little son whom both he and his wife worshipped.

But, unknown to the great majority of his fellow-citizens, Bernays was a profoundly un-happy and dissatisfied man—wretched in the one relationship that is all-important in adult life. William Bernays and Julia, his wife, each attractive, each clever, and each with a high if different ideal of duty, were utterly unsuited the one to the other.

Julia Bernays, the daughter óf a noted Belgian statesman, was a refined, high-strung, and austere-natured woman. True, she was beautiful, but beautiful—so her husband had once described her to a member of his own family—as a statue is beautiful.

The marriage had been arranged in the French fashion, but the two young people, well suited by birth, fortune, and age, had seemed much attracted to each other—Bernays, indeed, fell passionately in love with his future wife.

From the day of the wedding, however, the bridegroom's jovial, familiar ways offended and displeased his bride ; and after about a year of disunion, and of the discomfort that such disunion brings, they actually discussed the possibility of a separation.

But already the little son whom they both loved with a jealous love was born, and for the sake of their child, and because neither would consent to giving him up, in any real sense, to the other, they agreed to adjust their secret differences so far as to continue living in an outwardly friendly manner under the same roof.

Of this foolish and unnatural bargain ill was sure to come, and it soon did come in the shape at which the lawyer's acquaintances hinted among themselves when Bernays disappeared so suddenly and mysteriously from his home and usual haunts. The lawyer became frequently unfaithful to his wife, but in a furtive, shamed fashion which left it possible for those about them to hope and suppose that she knew nothing of these outrages on her wifely dignity. Outwardly William and Julia were on good and even cordial terms, and they kept the secret of their disunion hidden from everyone save certain very near relatives and friends.

But a worse and an infinitely less-to-be-expected complication than Bernays' light conduct had followed the arrangement entered into by the husband and wife—that arrangement which made them strangers under one roof.

Indeed, what had come to pass even before the disappearance of William Bernays may well inspire a Browning yet unborn to write another " Ring and the Book."

II

In the same town of Antwerp, united to the Bernays family by ties of long acquaintance rather than intimacy, lived a widow lady named Peltzer. She was the proud mother of three handsome sons, each of whom was very popular with the town folk.

In due course all the young Peltzers set out to carve their fortune, and Armand, a brilliant engineer, eldest and cleverest of the band of brothers, went off to America, where he was soon well on the way to prosperity.

He met, however, with one rebuff from Fate. He married a charming girl, whom he had the misfortune to lose after a very few years. She left him, however, a little daughter.

The two younger Peltzers stayed at home and engaged together in business. But they did not prosper as Armand had prospered, and there came a day when bankruptcy—and, what was even more terrible to this honourable family, a fraudulent bankruptcy—stared the partners in the face.

The mother cabled the news to her eldest born, and Armand, without losing a day, left his work and his happy, successful life in America, and hurried home in order to save his two brothers.

The engineer had lost touch with what was going on in his native place, and when he asked in the town to what lawyer he should address himself in the difficult task before him, everyone replied: " Go to William Bernays ! He is the only man who can get your brothers out of their dreadful scrape."

To William Bernays, Armand Peltzer accordingly went, and, thanks to the clever lawyer, the two young men came out of their trouble

with honour, if not with fortune saved, and
Armand ultimately found Léon, the cleverer of
his brothers, a good post in America.

But he himself lingered on in Antwerp. He
was in no hurry to go back to his adopted
country. He had brought his little girl with
him, and the presence of her son and her granddaughter made his mother a happy woman.

He struck up a great friendship with Bernays,
the lawyer who had saved his brothers from
dishonour. Armand Peltzer was very grateful
to William Bernays, and, as the engineer was
a clever man, and an agreeable talker, the two
soon became almost inseparable.

But what was surprising to those sufficiently
interested in other people's business to take
heed of such a thing was that Madame Bernays
—the beautiful, reserved Julia—also became on
terms of real friendship with Armand Peltzer.
She welcomed him as she did no other of her
husband's intimates to her house, and she took
a close and tender interest in his little girl. As
to him, we can perhaps guess what he felt as he
gradually grew to find himself on terms of close
friendship with

A lady, young, tall, beautiful, strange and sad.

Very soon the engineer became what a man
so often becomes when he is on friendly terms
with a husband and wife—the confidant, the

adviser, and the sympathiser of both. Both,
to him, broke their wise rule of silence, and he
listened to the expansive, over-frank complaints
and grievances of William, the aggrieved
husband, and heard with eager, respectful
sympathy the more reticent confidences of
William's lovely and now neglected wife.

The position of such a friend—of a man, that
is, who is intimate with a husband and a wife
who have ceased to be intimate with each other—
is very difficult and delicate. For such cases the
French have an excellent proverb, which runs:
" Between the tree and the bark do not try to
thrust thy finger."

Armand Peltzer certainly did his best, early
in the acquaintance, to bring William and Julia
together again ; but his efforts, as anyone but
an eager young man would have known they
would be, were quite unsuccessful. Indeed, his
efforts only ended by widening the breach between the lawyer and his wife. Soon Armand
himself became devotedly—he always declared,
on oath and in the most solemn way, platoni-
cally—attached to Julia Bernays, to the wife of
the man who had proved himself, since Peltzer's
return home to Antwerp, his best and wisest
friend.

Time went on, and still the young engineer
lingered in the town where his mother lived.
And only Madame Peltzer, with her keen

mother instinct of what ailed her son, suspected who it was that was keeping him there.

It is on record that she warned him of his peril, but that he angrily repudiated her suspicions. True, he was constantly in the Bernays' house; but if he paid long calls on Julia during William's business hours, he spent even longer hours in the lawyer's office, and the two men were always together in their spare time.

But there came a day when some cruel, mischief-making human being—it is said to have been the nurse of Madame Bernays' little boy— wrote an anonymous letter to William Bernays, asserting that his best friend, Armand Peltzer, was in love with Madame Bernays, and that all the gossips in Antwerp were talking about it.

Now Bernays, in spite, or perhaps because, of his wife's cold aloofness and his own secret flirtations, still loved his Julia quite sufficiently to be, or to become, violently jealous of her. The anonymous letter filled him with rage and suspicion, and instead of putting the coarse epistle into the fire, as he ought to have done, he kept it to show to his own family, and he wrote the following letter to Armand Peltzer:

Armand:
In spite of our friendship, I have to acquaint you with a painful but inevitable decision. I have received an anonymous letter concerning your friendship with Julia,.

and it is clear that I must safeguard the honour of my name. As your intimacy with my wife and myself causes low gossip, I must ask you to give up coming to our house.

My wife and I will henceforth live for our child. You also have the good fortune to be a father; I wish you and your child all possible happiness. Let us never associate our children with our misfortunes.

I beg of you, Armand, not to answer this letter. I am too unhappy, too shaken, to bear any discussion concerning the painful subject. Believe me, it hurts me greatly to break with an old and what has become an only intimate friendship; but I am sure that you will agree with me that, for both our sakes, it were better so.

I bid you farewell.

WILLIAM.

On the receipt of this letter Armand hurried round and insisted on seeing Bernays. He swore on what he held most sacred in the world—his child's life and his mother's honour—that he had never said a word to Julia that a brother might not have said, and further, that he regarded her with the highest veneration. His words bore such an accent of truth that William, ashamed of his base suspicions, humbly asked Armand's pardon. Nay, more; he asked him to come and dine with him and with Julia the same night.

But the happy spell of innocent friendship between these three people had been broken. The lawyer went on receiving anonymous letters, and there came an evening when William thought that he detected a meaning and a secret smile between Armand and Julia.

He got up from the table, and, making—poor fool that he was—a violent scene in front of his wife, plainly told the other man that he could not bear his presence in his house any longer; and the next day he wrote the engineer a letter in which he tried once more to express exactly what he felt about the whole painful matter:

Armand:

After all that has come and gone, I have to think, not only of what may be true, but of what may be said, and in view of the anonymous letters I continue to receive, I cannot doubt that your frequent presence in my house is making people talk. I beg you, therefore, in the name of my honour and of Julia's good name, to discontinue your visits. My wife and I live only for our son. You also have the good fortune to have a child. Let us never associate either of our children with any scandal. Pray send no reply to this letter. Neither speak nor write to me about it. I am very sorry to have to sever our friendship, but I am sure that you will feel with me that we can pursue no other course.

10

Would that Armand Peltzer had obeyed the entreaty contained in this letter! It was, it must be admitted, a wise, a dignified, and, on the whole, a high-minded letter for a husband to write to the friend who, now that the scales had fallen from that husband's eyes, was seen by him to cherish a violent if a still respectful passion for his wife.

But Peltzer did not receive the letter at all in the spirit in which it had been written. He chose to read in it an intolerable insult. His friendship for the lovely, ·neglected young married woman had become to him the noblest, as well as the most absorbing, passion of his lonely life. Nay, more; he told his mother— his unhappy, anxious mother, who alone had suspected the truth almost before he knew it himself—that it would be ignoble on his part to give up his acquaintance with Julia Bernays.

Armand sent no answer to his old friend's letter, but he evidently communicated its purport to his old friend's wife; and she, angered, as will be understood by every woman who reads this strange and terrible story of love and hate, by what she took to be a most unworthy and shameful suspicion, went straight to her husband with the news that she now intended to obtain a divorce.

Bernays was bewildered and horrified by his wife's threat. He eagerly declared that he did not suspect and never had suspected Julia, and further that he even acquitted her of imprudence.

He confessed to a morbid fear of gossip and scandal. Were he and Julia, he asked reproach-fully, to part because of a foolish quarrel brought about by scurrilous anonymous letters? Was their home, all the dignity of their joint life, to come to an end just as their little son was growing old enough to understand what it means when a father and mother are divorced and the home is broken up?

Nay, more, thoroughly sobered by his wife's cold anger and virtuous indignation, William Bernays sought out his own and Julia's lifelong friend, the President of the Belgian High Court, Monsieur Longé.

To this wise old man he told the whole story, and how little the whole story seemed when it was put in plain language!

Monsieur Longé reasoned with Julia. He showed her that her sudden wish for a divorce was cruel to her child, and finally, with her consent, he drew up a sort of informal deed which both husband and wife were to sign and leave with him.

The first clause in the deed expressed Bernays' great regret at having unjustly accused his wife of indiscreet behaviour, and recognized the utter falsity of the accusation.

The second clause arranged that the husband

and wife should each inhabit a separate suite of apartments in the same house, and it even stipulated that their meals should be served apart unless, for the benefit of the child, either thought it advisable that they should meet occasionally at luncheon.   Together, also, they were to settle everything that concerned the little boy's health and education.

Madame Bernays, on her side, undertook to behave exactly as a wife should behave when her husband's friends came to the house.   But she stipulated that she was *to be perfectly free as to the choice of her friends.*

Finally, husband and wife agreed never to engage in painful discussions the one with the other, and to allow Monsieur Longé to arbitrate between them in case of any difference of opinion.

Julia Bernays' first act after the deed had been signed was to invite Armand Peltzer to dinner.

She was " *to be perfectly free as to the choice of her friends*," and it seemed to this wrong-headed woman that her womanly honour demanded of her that she should break the spirit, while obeying the letter, of the new agreement into which she and her husband had entered together.

As soon as Bernays heard what she had done

he made matters worse by preparing to break the letter of the law to which he had agreed.

" No," he said firmly ; " I will not tolerate the presence of Armand Peltzer in our house. His coming is bound to lead to fresh difficulties and troubles."

Thus, before the ink on their signatures was well dry, husband and wife were disregarding, the one the spirit and the other the letter, of the deed.

In vain their trusted friend, Monsieur Longé, implored Julia to give way, and told her that she was doing very, very wrong. She insisted, on the contrary, that she was doing right, and that only Armand Peltzer's presence in their house would make her feel that her husband no longer suspected her.

She also considered it her duty to inform Armand of what had followed on her invitation to him. This naturally set him afire too. He sat down and wrote an angry, and yet it must be admitted a dignified, letter, in his turn, to William Bernays :

William :
After the interview in which you begged me to forgive your unjust and dishonouring suspicions of your wife and of myself, I thought all was right again between us. But there came, as you know, further trouble. I learn that in the deed you and your wife have signed it is expressly stipulated that

Julia may choose her own friends. Now she chooses me to be her friend, and frankly asks you to receive me as such. You refuse to do so, and that is a gross insult to me.

Your wife, who has a noble heart, is devoted to my little daughter. In her interest, and in the interest of my child, also in the interest of yours, I consent to hold out my hand and again to forgive you. Thus will be prevented any foolish talk about the noble and pure-minded woman who bears your name. You have indeed acted ill to your only friend—that is, to me, and I can never, never hope to forget your conduct in this matter.

Bernays returned this letter unopened, and the same evening Armand Peltzer sent the lawyer a formal challenge to a duel.

Now, Bernays, either because he was physically a coward, or because he dreaded the wave of talk that a duel always provokes in foreign society, was horrified by the receipt of Armand's challenge, and he actually sent his one-time friend a written apology for what he termed his "unjust suspicions."

Bernays, however, remained firm as to the one thing that really mattered to them all, and on which his wife and Armand Peltzer were determined to make him yield. Though he seemed willing to meet his wife half way as to almost everything concerning their joint life, he would

not give in about this one matter. He refused
to receive, or to allow her to receive, visits from
Armand Peltzer.

In a letter to the venerable President of the
Belgian High Court, a personal friend, it will be
remembered, of both his own parents and those
of Julia, Bernays endeavoured to explain exactly
how he felt about the matter :

> I am willing to accept all my wife's con-
> ditions and to observe them faithfully, with
> one exception ; I must refuse to receive
> Peltzer as a friend. Julia must not push
> me too far. She must not ask me to do
> what is above my strength. Unless the
> fact is pointed out to them, no one among
> our friends will notice whether we receive
> Peltzer or not. As long as Julia is in my
> house, living with me as my wife, she will
> neither be suspected nor talked of un-
> pleasantly. It is absurd to say that for her
> sake I should put up with the society of
> Monsieur Peltzer ; it would only lead to
> fresh trouble.

Peltzer could not make up his mind to this
complete separation from the woman he had
grown to love with a love which, as he always
solemnly declared, though absolutely pure, was
none the less ardent and absorbing. At the end
of a month of separation he wrote the following
letter to Bernays:

William :

I understand that you have signed an agreement by which you allow your wife complete freedom in the matter of receiving her friends. Further, you will remember having told me how very sorry you were for your unjust and ignoble suspicions. How amazed am I now to learn that you have made up your mind to a brutal and violent rupture between us! I might have challenged you to a duel, and I felt greatly tempted to do so ; but that would have made talk, and would have greatly injured the reputation of your wife, whom I respect and esteem. I did, however, ask my brother to arrange an interview between us. We could then have had a frank and loyal explanation. You refused ; thus confirming your first insult.

For the sake of Madame Bernays, whose noble character I venerate, and because of the gratitude I shall always feel for her kindness to my little girl, I still consent to meet you and to be seen in public with you. In that way we will both avoid being parties to a low and infamous machination which has had for object that of attacking the name of a woman who is, above all women, high-minded and pure.

ARMAND PELTZER.

This letter Bernays sent back unopened to the writer, and to a friend the barrister wrote : " I cannot tell you the hatred and contempt I feel for that man!" And to the same friend he sent a good many documents—various letters he had had from his wife, and so on.

Very soon the position between the husband and wife became so strained that Bernays, at last utterly disheartened, begged his wife, in his turn, to consent to a divorce for incompatibility of temper. But, to the great surprise of the few who were in their secret, Madame Bernays now absolutely refused to consider the question of a divorce.

When we think over and try to pierce the psychological mystery which is perhaps the most extraordinary feature of this extraordinary story, this final refusal of Julia to free herself from her husband is seen to have played a great and sinister rôle in the dread drama that followed.

And yet, who can doubt that had Julia Bernays desired to marry Armand, who by this time was madly in love with her, and for whom she seems to have cherished a very warm feeling of friendship, nothing would have been easier than for her to accomplish her purpose.

But in that case Julia would have had to give up her little son, or, at the best, to have shared him with her husband. According to the French and Belgian law, after a divorce has been granted, the father and mother of any child issued of the

10*

dissolved marriage have a right to their child's companionship for alternate months of each year.

Julia Bernays wrote to her old and trusted friend, President Longé:

> I entirely refuse to divorce William, because to do so would partially separate me from my child. I know my duty as my boy's mother, and it is a duty made the more incumbent on me owing to my profound contempt for the man who has behaved to me as Monsieur Bernays has done. He refused to defend my honour when it was odiously and basely challenged, and if he dares to institute a suit for divorce I shall know how to defend myself.

And so once more these unhappy people attempted to live together for the sake of their child and his future; and if Armand Peltzer had played a manly part and had gone away, as many a man situated as he was situated has done, all would have been, if not well, at least unshadowed by a terrible crime.

III

But human nature is a strange and complicated thing. Armand Peltzer had persuaded himself that his love for Julia Bernays was a noble passion of pity for an innocent woman hardly used by fate. Deep in his heart he knew that he loved her ; he desired ardently to marry her, and he wished that she should be free to consider him kindly.

When he found that her love for her child made divorce impossible to her, it became clear to him that there was but one way—albeit an awful and a dangerous way—in which to cut through the tangle in which he found himself.

William Bernays must be made to disappear, and the secret of his disappearance must be solved by the discovery of his death. Only as a widow could Julia become a happy wife.

And Bernays, as we know, did disappear. He took train to Brussels on that bright, sunny January day, and thenceforth he seemed obliterated as completely as if he had never existed.

An exhaustive hunt for the vanished man took place all over the continent of Europe. But the mystery remained impenetrable, and there followed nine long days of anxious waiting on the part of Julia, her little boy, and Bernays' own family, which included an aged father and mother.

On the last of the nine days the Chief of the Brussels police received the following strange letter. It was dated Basle, and ran as follows :

Sir :

I am horrified to learn in the papers that the letter that I wrote you—indeed, the letters I wrote you, for I have written two

—did not reach you! Monsieur William Bernays, alas! has not disappeared. He is dead. He was killed by accident in my Brussels office, 159, Rue de la Loi. The accident was entirely my fault—or, rather, the fault of my carelessness. He came to see me by appointment to talk over an important business matter. There was a pistol lying on my desk, and I foolishly took it up and began playing with it. Monsieur Bernays had already turned to leave the room when the trigger went off, and, to my intense horror, Monsieur Bernays fell dead at my feet. I thought—I hoped he was only wounded, but soon, alas! I saw that he was dead—and dead by my hand!

My first impulse was to send for the police. Then I remembered how very awkward and unpleasant would be my own position. I am an American, without a single friend or acquaintance in Brussels.

I therefore made up my mind that I had better leave Belgium and communicate with the police from a distance. I did so. But my letters seem to have miscarried. I am now very sorry that I behaved so foolishly. Still, I shall be able to prove that all I say is true, and I beg you to tell Monsieur Bernays' unfortunate family how deeply I sympathise with them, and how terribly sorry I am at having been the involuntary cause of his death.

I am, Sir, your obedient servant,

HENRY VAUGHAN.

Henry Vaughan ! Who was Henry Vaughan ? No trace of him could be found in the hotel registers of the town, and at first (so unlikely and unreal did the contents of this letter seem to be) the police took it to be one of those letters, often quite intelligently worded, which always follow on the commission of any widely advertised crime or disappearance, and which are the work of foolish or morbid practical jokers.

Still, as Rue de la Loi is a well-known street, it was thought worth while to send a couple of detectives to the address.

They found No. 159 to be a large, respectable house let out in business offices, and, after a certain amount of search and of inquiry from the porter, they further discovered that an American named Henry Vaughan had indeed hired an office in the building. This, however, only confirmed their belief that the letter had been written by some practical joker who wished to annoy Henry Vaughan.

Giving no hint of their dread mission, the two men made their way to the room which they were told was occupied by the American.

They knocked. There was no answer. Quickly and quietly they forced the lock, and there, huddled up in an armchair in front of a large desk on which lay a pistol, sat William Bernays— dead. He had been killed by a shot from behind, for there was a deep wound in the back of his neck.

Everything in the office was in perfect order. Bernays' heavy overcoat and his hat still hung on a stand near the door. A good deal of blood had gushed out on to the thick carpet, and there was the imprint of a man's boot-sole in the dried and coagulated blood. But that, though a painful detail, was natural enough. It was odd, however, that Henry Vaughan, after the accident, should have picked the dead man up and sat him down in the chair. Still, perhaps, he had done so hoping that Bernays was still alive.

In the unfortunate lawyer's pocket was found a certain amount of money, and the following letter, which confirmed the mysterious American's story :

> *Sir,*
> By the favour of an English friend I have obtained your name and address. They tell me you are the best lawyer in Antwerp, as well as an authority on commercial and maritime matters. This is why I ask your assistance concerning the state of Belgian law as to the following points.

Then came a number of highly technical questions as to the Belgian commercial and navigation laws and usages.

The long letter concluded with the words :

> I shall be much obliged if you will kindly answer the above by return, for I am

engaged, as you will understand, on a very important piece of business. As an earnest of my wish to avail myself of your legal assistance, I enclose a hundred and fifty dollars. I am told you are conversant with English as well as French. Pray write to me in either language.

I am, sir, your obedient servant,

HENRY VAUGHAN.

Yes, the story told in Henry Vaughan's letter was borne out by the facts—indeed, it was probably true in every particular. After all, truth, especially in criminal matters, is often far stranger than fiction.

But had the lawyer really died as Henry Vaughan declared he had done? The position of the wound gave the lie to the story—unless, of course, which seemed very unlikely, Bernays had suddenly turned away and so received the shot in the back of his neck instead of in his breast.

At any rate, there was but one thing now to do, and that was to get hold of Henry Vaughan.

The police soon discovered that the mysterious American was known to quite a number of important people in Belgium. Traces were found of him, not only at Basle, where his letter had been posted, and where he had stayed at a good hotel for some time, but also in various

Belgian and German towns. He appeared to be, as he had said in his letter, an American man of business travelling, however, on behalf of an important business concern in Australia.

But what had happened to him after he had left Basle, which he had apparently done within an hour of posting his letter, remained an impenetrable mystery. In fact, it seemed fairly obvious that " Henry Vaughan " had taken the wise if not very noble course of leaving for America immediately after he had written the letter—that curious, prudently worded letter— telling of the dreadful thing that had happened to him.

IV

Days and weeks slipped by. The body of the unfortunate William Bernays had been brought home to Antwerp and buried, amid marks of widespread sorrow and esteem, while among the chief mourners walked Armand Peltzer.

Madame Bernays and her little son went into deep mourning, and began to live the quietest and most retired of lives.

And then suddenly anonymous letters, bearing the postmark of Antwerp, began to rain in on the Brussels police ! These letters indicated, in language that became plainer and plainer, that

a certain Armand Peltzer, an engineer who was
now courting Madame Bernays with a view to
persuading her to make a second marriage, had
had a deep interest in the death of William
Bernays. Nay, more; they suggested that the
letter signed "Henry Vaughan" should be
compared with the handwriting of Armand
Peltzer!

Again the Chief of the Brussels police thought
he was being hoaxed, the more so that a very
few inquiries in Antwerp made it clear that the
Peltzers were people of consequence and re-
spectability. It was also ascertained that at the
present time two sons were living with their
widowed mother—Armand, the distinguished
engineer, who had come so nobly to his brother's
help some years before, and Léon, one of the
brothers who had been in trouble. Léon, who
was making a good livelihood in America, had
come home on a holiday.

Still, in view of the fact that the Brussels
police had never been wholly satisfied as to how
Bernays had met his death, specimens of the
handwriting, not only of Armand Peltzer, but
also, incidentally, of his brother Léon, were
secretly procured.

A great, an overwhelming surprise, was in
store for the official in charge of the affair.

While it did not require an expert to see that
there was nothing in common between the hand-

writing of the mysterious American and Armand
Peltzer, the handwriting of Léon Peltzer and that
of " Henry Vaughan " were absolutely identical !

A few hours after this fact had been ascertained, the two brothers were arrested, to the
extreme amazement, even the wrath, of many
of their fellow-townsmen with whom they had
been popular from childhood onward.

And then there followed one of those close,
ruthless, brilliant investigations that have become
the glory of the modern detective forces of
France, America, and England.

Once a clue is found, their task is often
pitifully easy. But this time the law had as
antagonist a really able man who had thought
out every detail of his plot with marvellous
ingenuity. Had Léon possessed the intellectual
capacity that distinguished his eldest brother,
Armand would almost certainly now be living
an honoured citizen of Antwerp, the devoted and
happy husband of the beautiful Julia, widow of
his one-time attached friend, William Bernays.

Amazing, almost incredible, in its cold,
reasoned cleverness, was the story that was
gradually unrolled—and the more amazing in
that neither brother gave himself or the other
away. Not only did they each protest their
innocence, but they did more ; they behaved,
while in prison awaiting trial, in a way to convince some of those who saw them that they

were innocent and that their consciences were at ease.

And yet, as the links in the chain became slowly but surely joined up, Armand and Léon must have known, only too well, that their sinister plot had only miscarried through Léon's folly. Had he not written the letter signed " Henry Vaughan " with his own hand—had he, for instance, had it typewritten, the Brussels police would never have obtained the clue which finally led to the two brothers standing their trial for the murder of William Bernays.

V

According to the prosecution the following were the facts of the case :

Léon Peltzer, after the serious business troubles from which his eldest brother had so cleverly extricated him, had been for a while a rolling stone.

He had stayed for varying periods in Manchester, in London, and in Buenos Aires. At last he had settled down in New York in the employment of a big and respectable firm ; and it was there, on an October day some three months before Bernays' disappearance, that the young Belgian suddenly informed his employers that he must leave them at a moment's notice. The reason he gave was that a Canadian friend,

who had once been very good to him, had tele-
graphed for his help in a serious difficulty.

But Léon Peltzer did not go to Europe via
Canada. The 1st of November found him on
board the *Arizona*, bound for Liverpool, under
the false name of Prélat. He probably found a
letter waiting for him from his brother, for he
went straight on to Paris, and there met Armand,
and although both men stayed at the same hotel
they used different names.

They spent four days together in Paris, and
then Armand, who was throughout the directing
intelligence, and who evidently found in Léon a
very willing instrument, went home to Antwerp.

Léon Peltzer at once moved to another Paris
hotel, again changing his name. It was from
there that he went to a hairdresser, and, explaining that he was going to a fancy dress ball,
bought a wig and a false beard. He waited a
day or two, and then, on the day he said the ball
was to take place, he went back to the same
hairdresser from whom he had bought the wig
and beard, and had himself thoroughly well
"made up." He even went to the trouble of
having his face stained a dark olive colour.

When he finally left the shop, Léon Peltzer
was so entirely unlike his usual self that not his
own mother, or so he was assured, would have
known him. From a fair Belgian he had become
in appearance a South American Spaniard.

His next step was to write a letter to Armand, dated "November 18—San Francisco." This letter Armand showed to several family friends in Antwerp. In it the writer described his busy, prosperous life, and announced that he would soon come home for a short holiday.

But Léon stayed on in Paris some time longer, and there, under the name of Viberg, he bought seven revolvers and three boxes of ammunition. After doing this he destroyed everything— clothes, papers, and so on—that he had brought from America, and, under yet another new name —that of Valgrave—he purchased an entirely new outfit, including a quantity of good under-clothes, but all these were marked, by his order, in the name he finally adopted, that of Henry Vaughan.

Thus equipped with a new name and a new personality, that of a traveller for Messrs. Murray and Co., of Sydney, come to Europe to organize a new service of steamers between Bremen, Hamburg, Amsterdam, and Australia, Léon Peltzer started on a series of cleverly planned journeys.

" Henry Vaughan," the dark, bearded, middle-aged looking South American, left Paris on December 1, and for three weeks he travelled .all over Holland and Germany, staying, among other places, at Hamburg, at Bremen, and at Amsterdam, seeing a good many business people

—especially lawyers—and making all kinds of arrangements that had the appearance of being absolutely genuine.

He stayed in good hotels, and seemed to have plenty of money with which to entertain new business acquaintances.

Never, in the long history of murder as a fine art, was murder more intelligently, and in a sense more intellectually, planned than was that of William Bernays. Neither time nor money— the two accomplices that are generally lacking to the murderer—was absent from the sinister tryst. Indeed, had Léon Peltzer possessed a tithe of his brother Armand's intellect, the two would certainly have succeeded in the scheme so cleverly imagined and so carefully and patiently carried out.

The fact that there were so many lawyers ready to come forward and say that they knew Henry Vaughan quite well, and that he was a respectable business man, had been naturally instrumental in causing the Brussels police to drop all inquiries until there came the anonymous letter clues from Antwerp.

But to return to the doings of " Henry Vaughan." After having thus created for himself a new and honourable personality, the pseudo-American went to Belgium. He travelled about for a while, then settled down in Brussels. There he hired an office in the Rue de la Loi,

and he purchased, not only a certain amount of
office furniture, but also a thick carpet, and even
a pair of thick curtains to hang over the door.
He also remembered to get a hat-and-coat
stand. This was in order that Bernays, on
coming into the room, should hang up his heavy
overcoat, which, if he had kept it on, might have
deviated the course of the bullet.

As to what actually occurred on the morning
of the murder, it remains, and will always
remain, a mystery.

Was William Bernays shot by Léon Peltzer
or by Armand ? Many Belgians believe that the
engineer arranged to give himself the satisfaction
of killing the man whom he had come to regard
as his deadly enemy, for it was the imprint of
the sole of Armand's boot which was found in
the coagulated blood on the carpet.

According to the medical evidence, Bernays
was not killed in the arm-chair where he was
found. He was shot standing, and his body
probably remained on the floor for twenty-four
hours. Then either Léon or Armand, or possibly
both brothers, came back, and so arranged the
body as to make his death appear an accident.

But it may be objected that though this story
of all that may have happened is very cleverly
imagined, how was it *proved* that Armand
Peltzer was directly concerned in the murder ?
The boot-sole imprint would be a very slight

piece of evidence on which to condemn a man to death.

It is true that, owing to Armand's acute and foreseeing intelligence, and also thanks to his brother's steadfast loyalty, the police found it very difficult to involve the elder Peltzer in the net of proof as surely as he himself had drawn his enemy into his snare. It may be doubted if, but for the existence of telegraphy, they could have succeeded.

Armand was doomed when at last the police discovered the telegrams which the brothers exchanged when about to meet in Paris. In Paris the detective's task was easy, for the French hotel-keeper at once recognized Armand as the man who had stayed with him at the same time as Léon. During the whole of Léon's peregrinations through Holland, Germany, and finally Belgium, the brothers were in constant communication, almost daily telegrams passing between them, Armand using an assumed name, that of a woman.

Yet another fact which told terribly against the elder brother became known to the police. On December 23 he had begun practising pistol-shooting in his mother's house. Their neighbours complained of the noise, and Armand soon desisted from his strange diversion; but, hidden in a secret place, there were afterwards found a large number of cartridges which were proved to be those which Léon had bought in Paris.

It is a curious fact that none of the seven revolvers bought in France seems to have satisfied Armand as being suitable for his purpose, for Léon made a hurried journey from Brussels to London, and it was with a revolver bought from an English gun-maker that William Bernays was shot.

On the very morning of the murder the younger brother addressed to the elder the following telegram :

" Thanks for your charming proposal. I hope to see you Saturday.—Marie."

This, being interpreted, meant: " He has accepted my proposal: I hope to see him to-day."

Armand declared that it had been sent him by a woman whom he had met by chance, and with whom he had made an assignation. Unfortunately for him, the original draft of the telegram was found in the Brussels post-office, and it was in Léon's handwriting !

VI

When at last the two brothers were put on their trial, the case excited most extraordinary interest, not only in Belgium, but all over the Continent.

The trial lasted a whole month, and, as is the custom in France and Belgium, numberless witnesses were called who in America or in England would have been considered to have little or no connection with the case.

Practically all of the relatives of each of the parties—of the murdered man, of his wife, and of the two men in the dock—were heard at length, and even asked for their opinion on the affair.

Each of the brothers also gave in the witness-box his own explanation of what had taken place, and it is a curious and rather touching fact that the object of each seemed to be to guard and to exculpate the other.

" Is it likely," cried Armand, " that Léon, who had absolutely no interest in Bernays' death, should have murdered a man simply because I disliked him ? " And then, in eloquent language, he went on to assert the purity of his affection for Madame Bernays, much in the same noble words that Browning put in Caponsacchi's mouth when addressing the Judges :

You know this is not love, sirs—it is faith.

Léon also tried to shield his brother. " I shot William Bernays because he penetrated the disguise I had assumed in order to carry out a fraudulent bit of business," he declared coolly. " Is it probable, is it even conceivable, that my brother Armand should have desired to murder Bernays, considering that Madame Bernays had the power of divorcing her husband ? "

The most exciting moment of the trial came with the appearance of Julia Bernays in the witness-box.

Dressed in widow's weeds, her splendid golden hair tucked away out of sight, her large blue eyes red-rimmed with long weeping, she looked more ethereal, more spiritually beautiful than ever.

"I am here," she said in a firm, low voice, "not to accuse, but to forgive——" There was a pause, and then she went on: "It is my husband I try to forgive for his infamous conduct."

She denied, in the most moving and solemn way, that her feeling for Armand Peltzer had ever been anything but a pure and high-minded friendship—"and it is a friendship," she concluded, "which has never faltered, and which is as constant, true, and pure to-day as it ever was." And then she exchanged a long, sad, ardent glance with the fine-looking young man who stood, with folded arms, in the dock.

The two brothers were defended by the leading barristers of the day; but nothing could avail them in the face of the irrefutable evidence which had been pieced together as the result of Léon's one act of carelessness.

The verdict was never in doubt.

The judge asked the prisoners if they had anything to say.

"I have to say," replied Léon Peltzer eagerly,

"that I accept the condemnation. But my brother Armand is absolutely innocent, and the jury have committed a judicial crime in condemning him."

Armand, turning to the twelve men who had just pronounced his fate, cried in a loud voice:

" On the jury will lie for ever the curse of my child ! "

.